Foreword from the Publisher

Wiley's publishing vision for the Microsoft Official Academic Course series is to provide students and instructors with the skills and knowledge they need to use Microsoft technology effectively in all aspects of their personal and professional lives. Quality instruction is required to help both educators and students get the most from Microsoft's software tools and to become more productive. Thus our mission is to make our instructional programs trusted educational companions for life.

To accomplish this mission, Wiley and Microsoft have partnered to develop the highest quality educational programs for Information Workers, IT Professionals, and Developers. Materials created by this partnership carry the brand name "Microsoft Official Academic Course," assuring instructors and students alike that the content of these textbooks is fully endorsed by Microsoft, and that they provide the highest quality information and instruction on Microsoft products. The Microsoft Official Academic Course textbooks are "Official" in still one more way—they are the officially sanctioned courseware for Microsoft IT Academy members.

The Microsoft Official Academic Course series focuses on *workforce development*. These programs are aimed at those students seeking to enter the workforce, change jobs, or embark on new careers as information workers, IT professionals, and developers. Microsoft Official Academic Course programs address their needs by emphasizing authentic workplace scenarios with an abundance of projects, exercises, cases, and assessments.

The Microsoft Official Academic Courses are mapped to Microsoft's extensive research and job-task analysis, the same research and analysis used to create the Microsoft Technology Associate (MTA) and Microsoft Certified Technology Specialist (MCTS) exams. The textbooks focus on real skills for real jobs. As students work through the projects and exercises in the textbooks, they enhance their level of knowledge and their ability to apply the latest Microsoft technology to everyday tasks. These students also gain resume-building credentials that can assist them in finding a job, keeping their current job, or furthering their education.

The concept of life-long learning is today an utmost necessity. Job roles, and even whole job categories, are changing so quickly that none of us can stay competitive and productive without continuously updating our skills and capabilities. The Microsoft Official Academic Course offerings, and their focus on Microsoft certification exam preparation, provide a means for people to acquire and effectively update their skills and knowledge. Wiley supports students in this endeavor through the development and distribution of these courses as Microsoft's official academic publisher.

Today educational publishing requires attention to providing quality print and robust electronic content. By integrating Microsoft Official Academic Course products, *WileyPLUS*, and Microsoft certifications, we are better able to deliver efficient learning solutions for students and teachers alike.

Joseph Heider

General Manager and Senior Vice President

Welcome to the Microsoft Official Academic Course (MOAC) program for Database Fundamentals. MOAC represents the collaboration between Microsoft Learning and John Wiley & Sons, Inc. publishing company. Microsoft and Wiley teamed up to produce a series of textbooks that deliver compelling and innovative teaching solutions to instructors and superior learning experiences for students. Infused and informed by in-depth knowledge from the creators of Microsoft products, and crafted by a publisher known worldwide for the pedagogical quality of its products, these textbooks maximize skills transfer in minimum time. Students are challenged to reach their potential by using their new technical skills as highly productive members of the workforce.

Because this knowledge base comes directly from Microsoft, creator of the Microsoft Certified Technology Specialist (MCTS), and Microsoft Technology Associate (MTA) exams (www.microsoft. com/learning/mcp/mcts), you are sure to receive the topical coverage that is most relevant to your personal and professional success. Microsoft's direct participation not only assures you that MOAC textbook content is accurate and current; it also means that you will receive the best instruction possible to enable your success on certification exams and in the workplace.

▪ The Microsoft Official Academic Course Program

The *Microsoft Official Academic Course* series is a complete program for instructors and institutions to prepare and deliver great courses on Microsoft software technologies. With MOAC, we recognize that, because of the rapid pace of change in the technology and curriculum developed by Microsoft, there is an ongoing set of needs beyond classroom instruction tools for an instructor to be ready to teach the course. The MOAC program endeavors to provide solutions for all these needs in a systematic manner in order to ensure a successful and rewarding course experience for both instructor and student—technical and curriculum training for instructor readiness with new software releases; the software itself for student use at home for building hands-on skills, assessment, and validation of skill development; and a great set of tools for delivering instruction in the classroom and lab. All are important to the smooth delivery of an interesting course on Microsoft software, and all are provided with the MOAC program. We think about the model below as a gauge for ensuring that we completely support you in your goal of teaching a great course. As you evaluate your instructional materials options, you may wish to use this model for comparison purposes with available products:

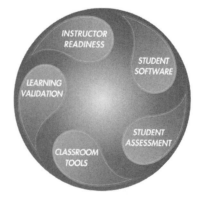

Microsoft® Official Academic Course

Database Fundamentals, Exam 98-364

WILEY

Credits

EDITOR	Bryan Gambrel
DIRECTOR OF SALES	Mitchell Beaton
EXECUTIVE MARKETING MANAGER	Chris Ruel
MICROSOFT SENIOR PRODUCT MANAGER	Merrick Van Dongen of Microsoft Learning
EDITORIAL PROGRAM ASSISTANT	Jennifer Lartz
CONTENT MANAGER	Micheline Frederick
PRODUCTION EDITOR	Amy Weintraub
CREATIVE DIRECTOR	Harry Nolan
COVER DESIGNER	Jim O'Shea
TECHNOLOGY AND MEDIA	Tom Kulesa/Wendy Ashenberg

Cover photo: Credit: Matthias Hombauer photography/Getty Images, Inc.

This book was set in Garamond by Aptara, Inc. and printed and bound by Bind Rite Robbinsville. The cover was printed by Bind Rite Roobinsville.

Microsoft, ActiveX, Excel, InfoPath, Microsoft Press, MSDN, OneNote, Outlook, PivotChart, PivotTable, PowerPoint, SharePoint, SQL Server, Visio, Visual Basic, Visual C#, Visual Studio, Windows, Windows 7, Windows Mobile, Windows Server, and Windows Vista are either registered trademarks or trademarks of Microsoft Corporation in the United States and/or other countries. Other product and company names mentioned herein may be the trademarks of their respective owners.

The example companies, organizations, products, domain names, e-mail addresses, logos, people, places, and events depicted herein are fictitious. No association with any real company, organization, product, domain name, e-mail address, logo, person, place, or event is intended or should be inferred.

The book expresses the author's views and opinions. The information contained in this book is provided without any express, statutory, or implied warranties. Neither the authors, John Wiley & Sons, Inc., Microsoft Corporation, nor their resellers or distributors will be held liable for any damages caused or alleged to be caused either directly or indirectly by this book.

Founded in 1807, John Wiley & Sons, Inc. has been a valued source of knowledge and understanding for more than 200 years, helping people around the world meet their needs and fulfill their aspirations. Our company is built on a foundation of principles that include responsibility to the communities we serve and where we live and work. In 2008, we launched a Corporate Citizenship Initiative, a global effort to address the environmental, social, economic, and ethical challenges we face in our business. Among the issues we are addressing are carbon impact, paper specifications and procurement, ethical conduct within our business and among our vendors, and community and charitable support. For more information, please visit our website: www.wiley.com/go/citizenship.

ISBN 978-0-470-88916-9

Printed in the United States of America

10 9 8 7 6 5 4

www.wiley.com/college/microsoft *or*
call the MOAC Toll-Free Number: 1+(888) 764-7001 (U.S. & Canada only)

Illustrated Book Tour

▪ Pedagogical Features

The MOAC textbook for Database Fundamentals is designed to cover all the learning objectives for that MTA exam 98-364, which is referred to as its "lesson skill matrix." The Microsoft Technology Associate (MTA) exam objectives are highlighted throughout the textbook. Many pedagogical features have been developed specifically for the *Microsoft Official Academic Course* program.

Presenting the extensive procedural information and technical concepts woven throughout the textbook raises challenges for the student and instructor alike. The illustrated book tour that follows provides a guide to the rich features contributing to the *Microsoft Official Academic Course* program's pedagogical plan. The following is a list of key features in each lesson designed to prepare students for success as they continue in their IT education, on the certification exams, and in the workplace:

- Each lesson begins with an **Objective Domain Matrix**. More than a standard list of learning objectives, the Lesson Skill Matrix correlates each software skill covered in the lesson to the specific exam objective.

- Concise and frequent **Step-by-Step** instructions teach students new features and provide an opportunity for hands-on practice. Numbered steps give detailed, step-by-step instructions to help students learn software skills.

- **Illustrations**—in particular, screen images—provide visual feedback as students work through the exercises. These images reinforce key concepts, provide visual clues about the steps, and allow students to check their progress.

- Lists of **Key Terms** at the beginning of each lesson introduce Students to important technical vocabulary. When these terms are used later in the lesson, they appear in bold, italic type where they are defined.

- Engaging point-of-use **Reader Aids**, located throughout the lessons, tell students why a topic is relevant (*The Bottom Line*) or provide students with helpful hints (*Take Note*). Reader Aids also provide additional relevant or background information that adds value to the lesson.

- **Certification Ready** features throughout the text signal students where a specific certification objective is covered. They provide students with a chance to check their understanding of that particular MTA objective and, if necessary, review the section of the lesson where it is covered. MOAC offers complete preparation for MTA certification.

- **End-of-Lesson Questions:** The Knowledge Assessment section provides a variety of multiple-choice, true-false, matching, and fill-in-the-blank questions.

- **End-of-Lesson Scenarios:** Competency Assessment case scenarios and Proficiency Assessment case scenarios are projects that test students' ability to apply what they've learned in the lesson.

▪ Lesson Features

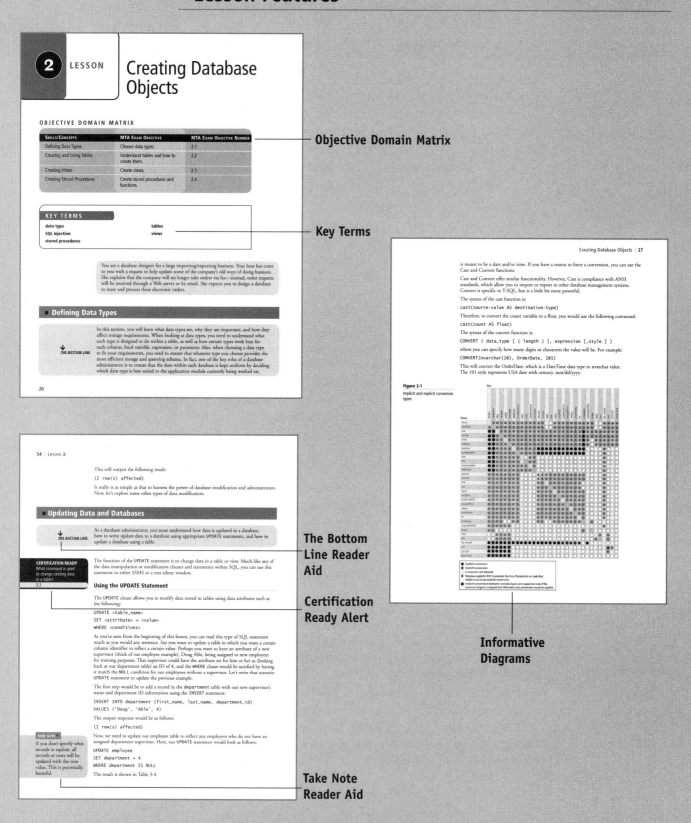

Objective Domain Matrix

Key Terms

The Bottom Line Reader Aid

Certification Ready Alert

Informative Diagrams

Take Note Reader Aid

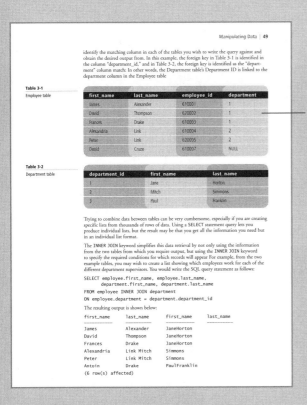

Easy-to-read Tables

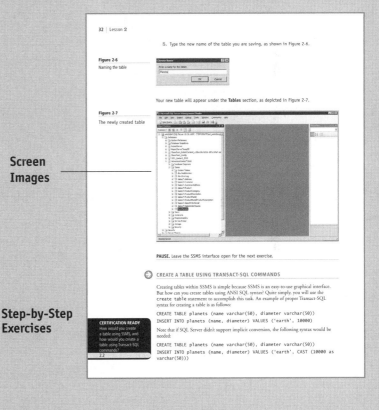

Screen Images

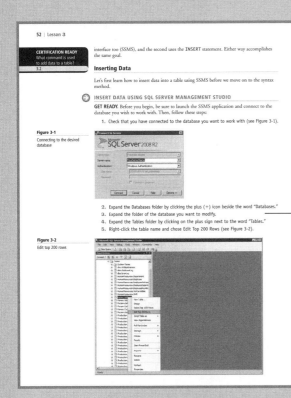

Step-by-Step Exercises

www.wiley.com/college/microsoft *or*
call the MOAC Toll-Free Number: 1+(888) 764-7001 (U.S. & Canada only)

38 | Lesson 2

Microsoft SQL Server already has hundreds of system-stored procedures so that you can perform basic functions. For example, you can use the Select Stored Procedure to retrieve or select rows from a database. Some of the more popular stored procedures will be covered in the next lesson including SELECT, INSERT, UPDATE, and DELETE.

Understanding SQL Injections

TAKE NOTE*
A SQL injection is an attack in which malicious code is inserted into strings to be passed on later when parsing or executing statements.

Before you learn the syntax statements for selecting, inserting, updating, and deleting data, you need to understand what a SQL injection is. In short, a *SQL injection* is an attack in which malicious code is inserted into strings that are later passed on to instances of SQL Server waiting for parsing and execution. Any procedure that constructs SQL statements should be reviewed continually for injection vulnerabilities because SQL Server will execute all syntactically valid queries from any source.

The primary form of SQL injection is a direct insertion of code into user-input variables that are concatenated with SQL commands and then executed. A less direct method of attack injects malicious code into strings that are destined for storage in a table or are considered metadata. When these stored strings are subsequently concatenated into the dynamic SQL command, the malicious code will be executed.

The injection process's function is to terminate a text string prematurely and append a new command directed from it; because the inserted command may have additional strings appended to it before it is executed, the malefactor terminates the injected string with a comment mark "—", making subsequent text ignored at execution time.

SKILL SUMMARY ────────────── — **Skill Summary**

IN THIS LESSON, YOU LEARNED THE FOLLOWING:

• A data type is an attribute that specifies the type of data an object can hold, as well as how many bytes each data type takes up.
• As a general rule, if you have two data types that differ only in how many bytes each uses, the one with more bytes has a larger range of values and/or increased precision.
• Microsoft SQL Server includes a wide range of predefined data types called built-in data types. Most of the databases you will create or use will employ only these data types.
• Exact numeric data types are the most common SQL Server data types used to store numeric information.
• int is the primary integer (whole number) data type.
• Precision (p) is the maximum total number of decimal digits that can be stored in a numeric data type, both to the left and to the right of the decimal point; this value must be at least 1 and at most 38. The default precision number is 18.
• money and smallmoney are Transact-SQL data types you would use to represent monetary or currency values. Both data types are accurate to 1/10,000th of the monetary units they represent.
• Approximate numeric data types are not as commonly used as other SQL Server data types. If you need more precision (more decimal places) than is available with the exact numeric data types, you should use the float or real data types, both of which typically take additional bytes of storage.
• The date and time data types, of course, deal with dates and times. These data types include date, datetime2, datetime, datetimeoffset, smalldatetime, and time.

Creating Database Objects | 39

• SQL Server supports implicit conversions, which can occur without specifying the actual callout function (cast or convert). Explicit conversions require you to use the functions cast or convert specifically.
• A regular character uses one byte of storage for each character, which allows you to define one of 256 possible characters; this accommodates English and some European languages.
• A Unicode character uses two bytes of storage per character so that you can represent one of 65,536 characters. This added capacity means that Unicode can store characters from almost any language.
• When you use a VAR element, SQL Server will preserve space in the row in which this element resides on the basis of on the column's defined size and not the actual number of characters in the character string itself.
• The Unicode character strings nchar and nvarchar can either be fixed or variable, like regular character strings; however, they use the UNICODE UCS-2 character set.
• The purpose of a table is to provide a structure for storing data within a relational database.
• A view is simply a virtual table that consists of different columns from one or more tables. Unlike a table, a view is stored in a database as a query object; therefore, a view is an object that obtains its data from one or more tables.
• A stored procedure is a previously written SQL statement that has been stored or saved into a database.
• A SQL injection is an attack in which malicious code is inserted into strings that are later passed on to instances of SQL Server for parsing and execution.

■ **Knowledge Assessment**

Fill in the Blank

Complete the following sentences by writing the correct word or words in the blanks provided.

1. Each _____, _____, expression, and _____ always has a related data type.
2. A bit is a Transact-SQL integer data type that can take a _____ of 1, 0, or NULL.
3. When you are defining the cost of a product, it is best to use the _____ data type.
4. It is important to consider your use of _____ data sets when building tables dependent on daylight saving time.
5. SQL Server supports _____ conversions without using actual callout functions (cast or convert).
6. A regular character uses _____ byte(s) of storage for each character, whereas a Unicode character requires _____ byte(s) of storage.
7. The data set char is of _____ length and has a length of _____ bytes.
8. The purpose of a table is to provide a(n) _____ for storing data within a relational database.
9. When creating a view, be sure to consider _____ in your design.
10. When querying a database, you can obtain faster results from properly _____ tables and views.

Knowledge Assessment

Case Scenarios

Manipulating Data | 59

■ **Competency Assessment**

Scenario 3-1: Using the SELECT Command

You have just been hired as a database administrator for the AdventureWorks Corporation. A network administrator wants to know how to extract information from the AdventureWorks database. Therefore, you need to answer the following questions:

1. What command would you use to display records from a table?
2. What command would you use to display a FirstName and LastName from the Users table?
3. What command would you use to display all records from the Member database and have it sorted by the Name column?
4. What command would you use to display all records from the Suppliers table that have the City of Sacramento?
5. What command would you use to display the CompanyName, ContactName, and PhoneNumber from the Suppliers table with Supplier ID greater than 1000?
6. What command would you use to display CompanyName, ContactName, and Phone Number from the Customers table for companies that have more than 100 employees and reside in the state of California?

Scenario 3-2: Deleting Data from Tables

After you and the network administrator review some records in the AdventureWorks database, the two of you decide to delete some old records. This scenario brings up the following questions:

1. What command would you use to remove all records from the Customer table where the age is less than 18?
2. What command would you use to remove all records from the Schools table that have enrollment less than 500?
3. What command would you use to remove all records from the Contact table that do not have a country of USA and at the same time free the space used by those records?
4. What command would you use to delete the Temp table?

■ **Proficiency Assessment**

Scenario 3-3: Manipulating Data Using SELECT and JOIN Statements

You are a database administrator for the AdventureWorks Corporation. Some confusion has arisen because the company's purchase orders are stored in two tables. Therefore, you need to write a query to join the PurchaseOrderHeader in the sample database, AdventureWorks, to itself in order to provide a list of purchase orders paired together. Each row includes two purchase orders that have identical vendors and shipping methods.

1. After opening SSMS and accessing the AdventureWorks database, what query would you use against the AdventureWorks database to display the ProductSubcategoryID and ProductCategoryID from the Production.ProductSub table that contain the word "Bike"? You also want to sort by Subcategory Name.
2. What query would you use to join the ProductCategory table to the ProductSubcategory table in order to retrieve the Name column from within the ProductCategory table?

Conventions and Features Used in This Book

This book uses particular fonts, symbols, and heading conventions to highlight important information and call attention to special steps. For more information about the features in each lesson, refer to the Illustrated Book Tour section.

CONVENTION	MEANING
↓ THE BOTTOM LINE	This feature provides a brief summary of the material to be covered in the section that follows.
CLOSE	Words in all capital letters indicate instructions for opening, saving, or closing files or programs. They also point out items you should check or actions you should take.
CERTIFICATION READY	This feature signals a point in the text where a specific certification objective is covered. It provides you with a chance to check your understanding of that particular MTA objective and, if necessary, review the section of the lesson where the objective is covered.
TAKE NOTE*	Reader Aids appear in shaded boxes found in your text. *Take Note* provides helpful hints related to particular tasks or topics.
X REF	These notes provide pointers to information discussed elsewhere in the textbook or describe interesting features that are not directly addressed in the current topic or exercise.
Alt + Tab	A plus sign (+) between two key names means that you must press both keys at the same time. Keys that you are instructed to press in an exercise will appear in the font shown here.
Example	Key terms appear in bold, italic font when they are defined.

Instructor Support Program

The *Microsoft Official Academic Course* programs are accompanied by a rich array of resources that incorporate the extensive textbook visuals to form a pedagogically cohesive package. These resources provide all the materials instructors need to deploy and deliver their courses. Resources available online for download include:

- The **MSDN Academic Alliance** is designed to provide the easiest and most inexpensive developer tools, products, and technologies available to faculty and students in labs, classrooms, and on student PCs. A free three-year membership is available to qualified MOAC adopters.

  Note: Microsoft Windows Server 2008, Microsoft Windows 7, and Microsoft Visual Studio can be downloaded from MSDN AA for use by students in this course.

- The **Instructor's Guide** contains solutions to all the textbook exercises and Syllabi for various term lengths. The Instructor's Guide also includes chapter summaries and lecture notes. The Instructor's Guide is available from the Book Companion site (http://www.wiley.com/college/microsoft).

- The **Test Bank** contains hundreds of questions in multiple-choice, true-false, short answer, and essay formats, and is available to download from the Instructor's Book Companion site (www.wiley.com/college/microsoft). A complete answer key is also provided.

- A complete set of **PowerPoint presentations** and images is available on the Instructor's Book Companion site (http://www.wiley.com/college/microsoft) to enhance classroom presentations. Approximately 50 PowerPoint slides are provided for each lesson. Tailored to the text's topical coverage and Skills Matrix, these presentations are designed to convey key concepts addressed in the text. All images from the text are on the Instructor's Book Companion site (http://www.wiley.com/college/microsoft). You can incorporate them into your PowerPoint presentations or use them to create your own overhead transparencies and handouts. By using these visuals in class discussions, you can help focus students' attention on key elements of technologies covered and help them understand how to use these technologies effectively in the workplace.

- When it comes to improving the classroom experience, there is no better source of ideas and inspiration than your colleagues. The **Wiley Faculty Network** connects teachers with technology, facilitates the exchange of best practices, and helps enhance instructional efficiency and effectiveness. Faculty Network activities include technology training and tutorials, virtual seminars, peer-to-peer exchanges of experiences and ideas, personal consulting, and sharing of resources. For details, visit www.WhereFacultyConnect.com.

DREAMSPARK PREMIUM—FREE 3-YEAR MEMBERSHIP AVAILABLE TO QUALIFIED ADOPTERS!

DreamSpark Premium is designed to provide the easiest and most inexpensive way for universities to make the latest Microsoft developer tools, products, and technologies available in labs, classrooms, and on student PCs. DreamSpark Premium is an annual membership program for departments teaching Science, Technology, Engineering, and Mathematics (STEM) courses. The membership provides a complete solution to keep academic labs, faculty, and students on the leading edge of technology.

Software available through the DreamSpark Premium program is provided at no charge to adopting departments through the Wiley and Microsoft publishing partnership.

Contact your Wiley rep for details.

For more information about the DreamSpark Premium program, go to Microsoft's DreamSpark website.

Note: Windows Server and SQL Server can be downloaded from DreamSpark Premium for use in this course.

■ Important Web Addresses and Phone Numbers

To locate the Wiley Higher Education Representative in your area, go to http://www.wiley.com/college and click on the *"Who's My Rep?"* link at the top of the page, or call the MOAC Toll-Free Number: 1 + (888) 764-7001 (U.S. & Canada only).

To learn more about becoming a Microsoft Certified Technology Specialist and about exam availability, visit www.microsoft.com/learning/mcp/mcp.

■ Additional Resources

Book Companion Web Site (www.wiley.com/college/microsoft)

The students' book companion site for the MOAC series includes any resources, exercise files, and Web links that will be used in conjunction with this course.

Wiley Desktop Editions

Wiley MOAC Desktop Editions are innovative, electronic versions of printed textbooks. Students buy the desktop version for up to 50% off the U.S. price of the printed text, and they get the added value of permanence and portability. Wiley Desktop Editions also provide students with numerous additional benefits that are not available with other e-text solutions.

Wiley Desktop Editions are NOT subscriptions; students download the Wiley Desktop Edition to their computer desktops. Students own the content they buy to keep for as long as they want. Once a Wiley Desktop Edition is downloaded to the computer desktop, students have instant access to all of the content without being online. Students can print the sections they prefer to read in hard copy. Students also have access to fully integrated resources within their Wiley Desktop Edition. From highlighting their e-text to taking and sharing notes, students can easily personalize their Wiley Desktop Edition as they are reading or following along in class.

■ About the Microsoft Technology Associate (MTA) Certification

Preparing Tomorrow's Technology Workforce

Technology plays a role in virtually every business around the world. Possessing a fundamental knowledge of how technology works and understanding its impact on today's academic and workplace environment is increasingly important—particularly for students interested in exploring professions involving technology. That's why Microsoft created the Microsoft Technology Associate (MTA) certification—a new entry-level credential that validates fundamental technology knowledge among students seeking to build a career in technology.

The Microsoft Technology Associate (MTA) certification is the ideal and preferred path to Microsoft's world-renowned technology certification programs, such as Microsoft Certified Technology Specialist (MCTS) and Microsoft Certified IT Professional (MCITP). MTA is positioned to become the premier credential for individuals seeking to explore and pursue a career in technology, or enhance related pursuits such as business or any other field where technology is pervasive.

MTA Candidate Profile

The MTA certification program is designed specifically for secondary and post-secondary students interested in exploring academic and career options in a technology field. It offers students a certification in basic IT and development. As the new recommended entry point for Microsoft technology certifications, MTA is designed especially for students new to IT and software development. It is available exclusively in educational settings and easily integrates into the curricula of existing computer classes.

MTA Empowers Educators and Motivates Students

MTA provides a new standard for measuring and validating fundamental technology knowledge right in the classroom with minimal impact on your budget and teaching resources. MTA helps institutions stand out as innovative providers of high-demand industry credentials and is easily deployed with a simple, convenient, and affordable suite of entry-level technology certification exams. MTA enables students to explore career paths in technology without requiring a big investment of time and resources, while providing a career foundation and the confidence to succeed in advanced studies and future vocational endeavors.

In addition to giving students an entry-level Microsoft certification, MTA is designed to be a stepping stone to other, more advanced Microsoft technology certifications, like the Microsoft Certified Technology Specialist (MCTS) certification.

Delivering MTA Exams: The MTA Campus License

Implementing a new certification program in your classroom has never been so easy with the MTA Campus License. Through the purchase of an annual MTA Campus License, there's no more need for ad hoc budget requests and recurrent purchases of exam vouchers. Now you can budget for one low cost for the entire year, and then administer MTA exams to your students and other faculty across your entire campus where and when you want.

The MTA Campus License provides a convenient and affordable suite of entry-level technology certifications designed to empower educators and motivate students as they build a foundation for their careers.

The MTA Campus License is administered by Certiport, Microsoft's exclusive MTA exam provider.

To learn more about becoming a Microsoft Technology Associate and exam availability, visit www.microsoft.com/learning/mta.

■ Activate Your FREE MTA Practice Test!

Your purchase of this book entitles you to a free MTA practice test from GMetrix (a $30 value). Please go to www.gmetrix.com/mtatests and use the following validation code to redeem your free test: **MTA98-364-069439B3D150.**

The **GMetrix Skills Management System** provides everything you need to practice for the Microsoft Technology Associate (MTA) Certification.

Overview of Test features:

- Practice tests map to the Microsoft Technology Associate (MTA) exam objectives
- GMetrix MTA practice tests simulate the actual MTA testing environment
- 50+ questions per test covering all objectives
- Progress at own pace, save test to resume later, return to skipped questions
- Detailed, printable score report highlighting areas requiring further review

To get the most from your MTA preparation, take advantage of your free GMetrix MTA Practice Test today!

For technical support issues on installation or code activation, please email support@gmetrix.com.

Acknowledgments

■ MOAC MTA Technology Fundamentals Reviewers

We'd like to thank the many reviewers who pored over the manuscript and provided invaluable feedback in the service of quality instructional materials:

Yuke Wang, University of Texas at Dallas

Palaniappan Vairavan, Bellevue College

Harold "Buz" Lamson, ITT Technical Institute

Colin Archibald, Valencia Community College

Catherine Bradfield, DeVry University Online

Robert Nelson, Blinn College

Kalpana Viswanathan, Bellevue College

Bob Becker, Vatterott College

Carol Torkko, Bellevue College

Bharat Kandel, Missouri Tech

Linda Cohen, Forsyth Technical Community College

Candice Lambert, Metro Technology Centers

Susan Mahon, Collin College

Mark Aruda, Hillsborough Community College

Claude Russo, Brevard Community College

David Koppy, Baker College

Sharon Moran, Hillsborough Community College

Keith Hoell, Briarcliffe College and Queens College—CUNY

Mark Hufnagel, Lee County School District

Rachelle Hall, Glendale Community College

Scott Elliott, Christie Digital Systems, Inc.

Gralan Gilliam, Kaplan

Steve Strom, Butler Community College

John Crowley, Bucks County Community College

Margaret Leary, Northern Virginia Community College

Sue Miner, Lehigh Carbon Community College

Gary Rollinson, Cabrillo College

Al Kelly, University of Advancing Technology

Katherine James, Seneca College

Brief Contents

Contents

Understanding Core Database Concepts

OBJECTIVE DOMAIN MATRIX

SKILLS/CONCEPTS	MTA EXAM OBJECTIVE	MTA EXAM OBJECTIVE NUMBER
Understanding Database Concepts	Understand how data is stored in tables.	1.1
Understanding Relational Databases	Understand relational database concepts.	1.2
Understanding Data Manipulation Language	Understand data manipulation language (DML).	1.3
Understanding Data Definition Language (DDL)	Understand data definition language (DDL).	1.4

KEY TERMS

constraints

Data Definition Language (DDL)

Data Manipulation Language (DML)

database (db)

database management system (DBMS)

database server

flat-type database

hierarchical database

index

relational database

SQLCMD

SQL Server Management Studio (SSMS)

table

Transact-SQL

XQuery

You are a newly hired junior accountant at a prestigious accounting firm. You have just been tasked with compiling a financial outlook for one of the company's largest clients, with a turnaround time of three weeks. One of the firm's partners feels that the firm isn't getting all the financial data it needs using its existing methods of information retrieval. Presently, the firm uses Excel spreadsheets to create financial outlooks and current financial positions for each of its clients. Upon receiving a total of 15 spreadsheets for the client in question, you quickly realize that without a better way of gathering the information you need, you will not be able to complete your project in the time allotted.

Understanding Database Concepts

THE BOTTOM LINE

Before you begin creating tables and other database elements, you must first understand what databases are and what valuable tools they can be. The benefits of choosing the right type of database will become apparent once the database is used in your company.

A *database (db)* is an organized collection of data, typically stored in electronic format. It allows you to input, organize, and retrieve data quickly. Traditional databases are organized by fields, records, and files.

To better understand what a database is, consider the telephone book as a simple example. If you had the telephone book stored on disk, the book would be the file. Within the telephone book, you would have a list of records—each of which contains a name, address, and telephone number. These single pieces of information (name, address, phone number) would each constitute a separate field.

Because a database can store thousands of records, it would be a chore if you had to open a table and go through each record one at a time until you found the record you needed. Of course, the process would be even more difficult if you had to retrieve multiple records.

Thankfully, you don't have to go through database records in this way. Rather, to retrieve data within a database, you run a database *query*, which is an inquiry into the database that returns information back from the database. In other words, a query is used to ask for information from a database.

If a database contains thousands of records with many fields per record, it may take even a fast computer a significant amount of time to search through a table and retrieve the requested data. This is where a database index comes in handy. An *index* is a data structure that improves the speed of data retrieval operations on a database table. The disadvantage of indexes is that they need to be created and updated, which requires processing resources and takes up disk space.

Databases are often found on *database servers* so that they can be accessed by multiple users and provide a high level of performance. One popular database server is Microsoft SQL Server. Database servers like SQL Server do not actually house graphical programs, word-processing applications, or any other type of applications. Instead, these servers are entirely optimized to serve only the purposes of the database itself, usually using advanced hardware that can handle the high processing needs of the database. It is also important to note that these servers do not act as workstations; they generally are mounted on racks located in a central data center and can be accessed only through an administrator's desktop system.

Microsoft SQL Server uses three types of files to store databases. Primary data files, which have an .mdf extension, are the first files created in a database and can contain user-defined objects, such as tables and views, as well as system tables that SQL Server requires for keeping track of the database. If the database becomes too large and you run out of room on your first hard disk, you can create secondary data files, which have an .ndf extension, on separate physical hard disks. The third type of file used in SQL Server is a transaction log file. Transaction log files use an .ldf extension and don't contain objects such as tables or views.

Most users do not access a database directly. Instead, they use a *database management system (DBMS)* to access it indirectly. A DBMS is a collection of programs that enables you to enter, organize, and select data in a database. For example, a ticket agent may run a ticket system program on his or her desk computer that in turn accesses a ticketing database.

There are three types of databases with which you should be familiar in order to make the appropriate choice when developing your own database tables:

- Flat-type databases
- Hierarchical databases
- Relational databases

Each database type has its own important design features.

Understanding Flat-Type Databases

Flat-type databases are simplistic in design. They are most commonly used in plain-text formats. Because their purpose is to hold one record per line, they make access, performance, and queries very quick. An example of this type of database would be what you would find in a .txt or .ini file.

Flat-type databases are considered "flat" because they are two-dimensional *tables* consisting of rows and columns. Each column can be referred to as a field (such as a person's last name or a product's ID number), and each row can be referred to as a record (such as a person's or product's information). The following is an example of a simple flat-type database in which a supply company has matched each customer with what he or she consistently orders for easy retrieval and reordering purposes:

```
id      customer    order
1       allen       notebook
2       smith       paper
3       dennis      pens
4       alex        ink cartridges
5       sloan       printer
```

Understanding Hierarchical Databases

A *hierarchical database* is similar to a tree structure (such as a family tree). In this database, each "parent" table can have multiple "children," but each child can have only one parent.

An example of a parent/child hierarchical database is shown in Table 1-1. This database applies to a department of four employees for which the company has just purchased new equipment. Note that one table holds the employee information, whereas the other table holds data about the newly purchased equipment. Here, the table at the top is the "parent," and the table on the bottom is the "child." If several such tables are linked together, the database's tables will start to form a tree structure in which each parent may have multiple child tables and each child table may in turn have children of its own, yet no single child table will have more than one parent.

Table 1-1

Hierarchical database showing parent and child tables

Parent Table

EMPNUM	FIRSTNAME	LASTNAME	DEPTNUM
100	Paul	Baker	101
101	Jane	Smith	101
102	Jim	Tate	101
103	Ed	Rosen	102

Child Table

SERIALNUM	TYPE	EMPNUM
30032334	Computer	100
4323452	Laptop	101
342342	Monitor	100
234322	Printer	100

In this example, the parent table holds the employee data. Each row or record provides an employee's information, including his or her employee number (EmpNum). The child table holds the computer equipment data, and the EmpNum column links each record to the parent table. It is important to note that each piece of equipment must be entered separately. Because we are using a hierarchical database, we can assign multiple computer devices to each employee.

Understanding Relational Databases

CERTIFICATION READY
How do relational databases differ from flat-type databases and hierarchical databases?
1.2

The last yet most important database type is the relational database. A *relational database* is similar to a hierarchical database in that data is stored in tables and any new information is automatically added into the table without the need to reorganize the table itself. Unlike in hierarchical databases, however, a table in a relational database can have multiple parents.

An example of a relational database is shown in Table 1-2. The first parent table shows the salespeople within a company, and the second parent table lists what product models are sold by the company. Meanwhile, the child table lists customers who have purchased models from the company; this child table is linked to the first parent table by the SalesNum and to the second parent table by the Model.

Table 1-2

Relational database showing two parent tables and one child table

Parent Table 1

SalesNum	FirstName	LastName	DeptNum
100	Paul	Baker	101
101	Jane	Smith	101
102	Jim	Tate	101'
103	Ed	Rosen	102

Parent Table 2

Model	Cost	Color
2200MX	$75000	Red
42CRS	$55000	Gray
4232DR	$60000	Red
2201MX	$80000	Blue

Child Table

FirstName	LastName	IDNum	Model	SalesNum
Pete	Wilson	1001	2200MX	100
Jim	Cline	1002	42CRS	101
Omar	Salize	1003	4232DR	103
Louise	Peterson	1004	2201MX	100

Understanding Database Fundamentals

A simple database with one table is similar to a spreadsheet that contains rows and columns. However, unlike a spreadsheet, a database allows you to store thousands of rows of data and then access that information more quickly than by reading a spreadsheet.

A spreadsheet is often the starting point for creating a database. With a spreadsheet, it's easy to create headings and start entering data. Adding, deleting, reordering, and formatting headings is simple, and you can easily sort the data under one or more headings. It's also easy to insert, delete, and filter rows matching one or more patterns under a heading.

Many databases will accumulate thousands of rows of data. Depending on your needs, you may wish to create additional tables to hold some of this information. In a spreadsheet, this would be the same as adding additional worksheets.

Spreadsheets, however, are designed for and limited to only thousands of rows per worksheet. Moreover, when a spreadsheet is opened, the whole file is loaded into the computer's memory—so if enough data is stored, the file may eventually fail to load due to insufficient memory. Suddenly, the benefits of using a spreadsheet start to decline. This is when switching to a database makes the most sense.

This comparison highlights three fundamental characteristics of databases:

- They are designed to store billions of rows of data.
- They are limited to the computer's available hard disk space.
- They are optimized to use all a computer's available memory to improve performance.

COMPARING WORKSHEETS TO DATABASE TABLES

As you probably already know, a spreadsheet can contain several worksheets, each of which stores logically grouped information in a tabular format. A worksheet is comparable to a database table, and the headings within it are comparable to the columns or fields within a database table. In a spreadsheet with multiple worksheets, such as that shown in Figure 1-1, each worksheet can be thought of as a different table that belongs to the same database.

Figure 1-1

Spreadsheet with multiple worksheets

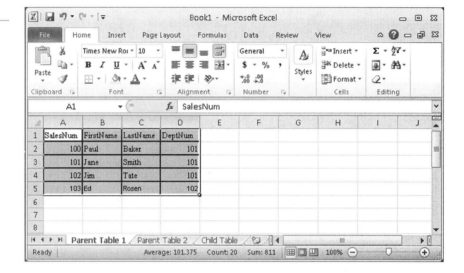

A worksheet column can contain data that might be blank; in such cases, a blank is stored as a Null in the database. A database table can be designed to either allow or disallow Nulls within a column.

UNDERSTANDING CALCULATED VALUES

In a spreadsheet, you can use formulas to calculate values from other information in the same row or column, as shown in Figure 1-2. A calculated value is essentially a value that results from the performance of some sort of calculation or formula on a specified input value. Databases can also be used to generate calculated values, either within the database, within the reports generated from the database, or within the application that is accessing the database.

Figure 1-2

Spreadsheet with calculated values

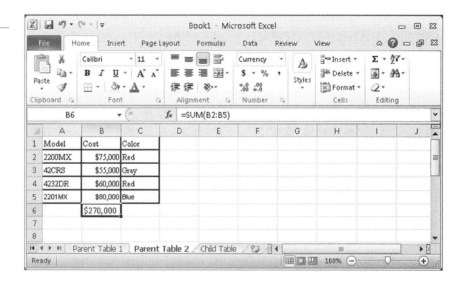

Understanding Relational Database Concepts

Before you design your first relational database, you must understand the elements that form this type of database and the terminology used to describe them.

To understand relational database models, think about the ways in which a table might relate to one or more other tables.

A relational database helps organize all the data from the various rows and columns of each table, as shown in Figure 1-3. Each column corresponds to one specific type of information you want to store in the database. As you look at the figure, envision each row corresponding to one record, and remember that one instance of each column and each table may be related to one or more other tables.

Figure 1-3

Basic database table

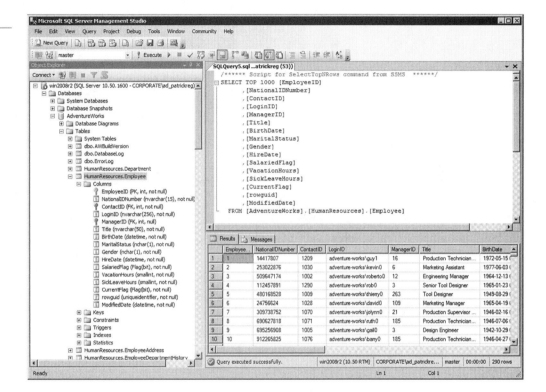

A relational database model would organize the data shown in Figure 1-3 into a database table that contains rows and columns, with each column corresponding to one attribute or type of information you want to store. In turn, each row would correspond to one record or one instance of each column.

INTRODUCING LANGUAGE ELEMENTS

Database objects are inherently divided into two broad categories: storage and programmability. A table is structured by columns and rows, and each column then stores data classified as a data type. Figure 1-4 shows sample column attributes for a database. There are a variety of data types to choose from, including built-in types and your own user-defined data types. Data types are discussed in greater detail in Lesson 2.

Figure 1-4

Database structure showing column attributes

TAKE NOTE*

Advanced databases, such as SQL Server, periodically analyze queries and create indexes as needed to optimize performance. You can find evidence of this by looking at the index in the database.

Constraints are limitations or rules placed on a field or column to ensure that data that is considered invalid is not entered. For example, if a person's age should be input, then the data that is entered must be a positive number—a person cannot have a negative age. A variety of constraints are available with SQL Server 2008, including the following:

- A unique constraint allows the database administrator to specifically identify which column should not contain duplicate values.
- A check constraint allows the administrator to limit the types of data a user can insert into the database.
- A default constraint is used to insert a default value into a column. If no other value is specified, the default value will be added to all new records.
- A not null constraint ensures that data is entered into a cell. In other words, the cell cannot be blank. It also means that you cannot insert a new record or update a record without adding a value to this field.
- The primary key constraint uniquely identifies each record in a database table. The primary key must contain unique values and it cannot contain NULL values. Each table should have a primary key, and each table can have only *one* primary key.
- A foreign key constraint in one table points to a primary key in another table.

For an example of database constraints, see Figure 1-5.

Figure 1-5

A database constraint

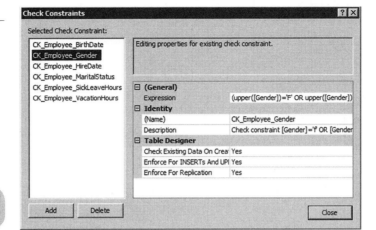

TAKE NOTE*

A foreign key is also known as a self-reference.

Columns marked as foreign keys can contain null values. This is *not* a desirable standard of practice, however, because it may be impossible to verify the constraints if a foreign key consists of two or more columns and contains null values. This means the integrity of your data cannot be guaranteed.

It is also possible for a foreign key constraint to reference columns in the same table; this is known as a self-reference. When a self-reference is used to query a table, this arrangement is now referenced as a self-join. As an example of a self-reference table, say you want to create a Generations table that contains names of people using columns named PersonID, PersonName, and MotherID. The mother is also a person stored in the Generations table, so you can create a foreign key relationship from the MotherID (the foreign key column) referencing PersonID (the primary key column).

Using the SQL Server Management Studio Interface

When you install Microsoft SQL Server, you also install the *SQL Server Management Studio (SSMS)*, which is the primary tool for managing the server and its databases using a graphical interface.

The central feature of SSMS is the Object Explorer, which allows users to browse, select, and manage any of the objects within the server (see Figure 1-6). SSMS can also be used to view and optimize database performance, as well as to create and modify databases, tables, and indexes.

Figure 1-6

SQL Server Management
Studio

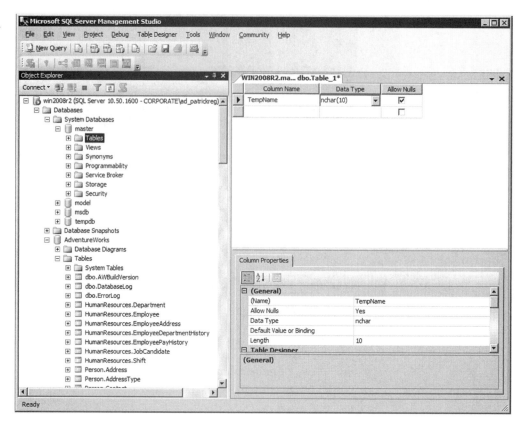

In addition, SSMS includes the Query Analyzer (see Figure 1-7), which provides a GUI-based interface to write and execute queries. The Query Analyzer supports the following:

- **XQuery** is a query and functional programming language that is designed to query collections of XML data.

Figure 1-7

Query Analyzer

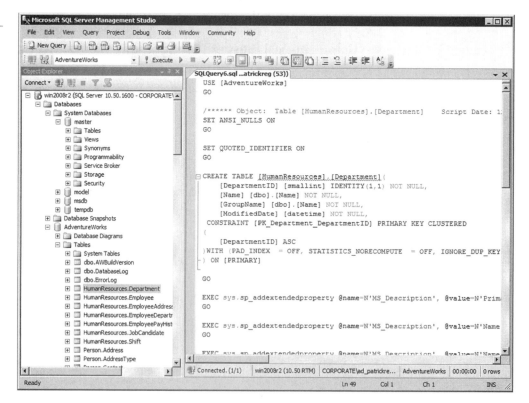

- *SQLCMD* is a command-line application that comes with Microsoft SQL Server and exposes the management features of SQL Server. It allows SQL queries to be written and executed from the command prompt. It can also act as a scripting language to create and run a set of SQL statements as a script. Such scripts are stored as .sql files, and they are used either for management of databases or to create the database schema during database deployment.
- *Transact-SQL* is the primary means of programming and managing SQL Server. It exposes keywords so that you can create and manage databases and their components and monitor and manage the server itself. When you use SSMS to perform an action or task, you are executing Transact-SQL commands.

Note that you must have SQL Server 2008 installed on your system before moving on to the next section.

 LOAD THE SSMS INTERFACE

GET READY. Before you begin these steps, be sure to launch SSMS.

1. Click the Start button, then click Microsoft SQL Server 2008 to expand the program selection.
2. Click SQL Server Management Studio. The Management Studio opens, displaying the Connect to Server dialog box.
3. Change the server connection details (if necessary) and click Connect. After you have configured the server setting correctly, the SQL Server Management Studio Interface will be visible.

➕ TROUBLESHOOTING

Your computer may not have the SSMS interface installed as part of the SQL Server 2008 program. If you cannot find the Management Studio tool when you look under Program Files, you may have to add it as a server installation update. To do this, insert the installation CD and click the Advanced button in the Components to Install window when it appears.

TAKE NOTE *
You can also install SQL Server Management Studio on any Windows desktop operating system so that you can remotely connect to and manage a SQL server.

PAUSE. Leave the SQL Server Management Studio open for the remainder of the lesson.

The SQL Server Management Studio can be used to perform most of the activities you are required to do and can be considered a "one-stop" tool.

 CREATE A DATABASE WITH THE SSMS INTERFACE

GET READY. Before you can start managing databases, you must first create them. To do so, follow these steps:

1. Open SSMS by clicking Start > All Programs > Microsoft SQL Server 2008 > SQL Server Management Studio.
2. Make sure the Database Engine is selected, then click the Connect button.
3. Click the plus sign (+) next to Databases to expand it.
4. Right-click Databases, then select New Databases from the menu that appears.
5. In the Database name field, type the name of the database you want to create. Then click the OK button.

DELETE A DATABASE WITH THE SSMS INTERFACE

GET READY. From time to time, you may want to remove databases that are no longer being used. To do so using the SSMS interface, follow these steps:

1. Open SSMS by clicking Start > All Programs > Microsoft SQL Server 2008 > SQL Server Management Studio.
2. Make sure the Database Engine is selected, then click the Connect button.
3. Click the plus sign (+) next to Databases to expand it.
4. Right-click the name of the database you want to delete, then select Delete from the menu that appears.
5. Select Close Existing Connections, then click the OK button.

It's important to note that SQL Server has an extensive help area. In addition, when you install SQL Server, you have the option to install Books Online and Server Tutorials. Therefore, if you want to find information about a certain option or command, you should start by checking these resources. Of course, if you still cannot find what you are looking for, don't be afraid to search the Internet.

■ Understanding Data Manipulation Language (DML)

↓ **THE BOTTOM LINE**   When creating databases, it is important to understand what language elements can do within your database structure.

CERTIFICATION READY
Which popular commands used with SQL are DML commands?
1.3

Data Manipulation Language (DML) is the language element that allows you to use the core statements INSERT, UPDATE, DELETE, and MERGE to manipulate data in any SQL Server tables. Core DML statements include the following:

- SELECT: Retrieves rows from the database and enables the selection of one or many rows or columns from one or many tables in SQL Server.
- INSERT: Adds one or more new rows to a table or a view in SQL Server.
- UPDATE: Changes existing data in one or more columns in a table or view.
- DELETE: Removes rows from a table or view.
- MERGE: Performs insert, update, or delete operations on a target table based on the results of a join with a source table.

When you use DML statements such as INSERT, UPDATE, DELETE, or MERGE, you need to realize that on the whole, they either succeed or fail. For example, if you were to try to insert 10,000 records into a table but violated one of the primary key or unique constraints, the entire 10,000 rows of records would roll back immediately and not one record would be inserted into the table. Similarly, if a DELETE statement violates a foreign key constraint (even in just one row), nothing would be deleted. Therefore, when using DML statements, you must query the table to verify that key constraints are met and your syntax is correct. The following section shows the correct syntax for working with constraints.

■ Understanding Data Definition Language (DDL)

 THE BOTTOM LINE   Data Definition Language (DDL) statements form part of the Transact-SQL portion of SQL Server and can be used to create database objects such as tables and views.

CERTIFICATION READY
What popular SQL commands are DDL commands?
1.4

Data Definition Language (DDL) is a subset of the Transact-SQL language; it deals with creating database objects like tables, constraints, and stored procedures. The interface used to create these underlying DDL statements is the SSMS user interface, as shown in Figure 1-8.

Figure 1-8

SQL Server Management Studio user interface

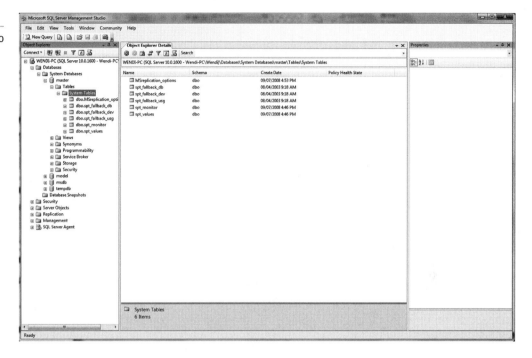

Using DDL Statements

The SSMS user interface allows you to visually design DDL statements. A DDL script statement task can always be completed through the SSMS user interface, but not all the options you may wish to use with the DDL script can be accomplished through this interface. Therefore, you must be familiar with the DDL statements USE, CREATE, ALTER, and DROP in order to create and manage tables, user-defined data types, views, triggers, functions, and stored procedures.

Although most DDL statements can be executed using the SSMS graphical interface, you still have more power, flexibility, and control when using DDL statements themselves. You can also use DDL statements to script tasks or activities that can be scheduled or executed as needed. Again, the six main DDL statements are as follows:

CERTIFICATION READY
What DDL command would you use to change the database content, and which would you use to create a table?
1.4

- USE: Changes the database context.
- CREATE: Creates a SQL Server database object (table, view, or stored procedure).
- ALTER: Changes an existing object.
- DROP: Removes an object from the database.
- TRUNCATE: Removes rows from a table and frees the space used by those rows.
- DELETE: Remove rows from a table but does not free the space used by those rows removed.

Let's go through each of these key DDL statements with further explanation and an example of each.

USE

One Transact-SQL command worth mentioning is the USE command. The USE command changes the database context to the specified database or database snapshot. In other words, when you perform commands on a particular database, you will likely have to enter the USE command to select the database first. For example, to select a database named TESTDB, you would execute the following command:

```
USE TESTDB
```

CREATE

The CREATE statement allows you to create a variety of database objects, including tables, views, and stored procedures. For instance, say you want to create a new table named Planets within a database named AdventureWorks. To do this, you would use the following sequence of commands:

```
USE [AdventureWorks]
GO
CREATE TABLE [dbo].[Planets](
    [IndvidualID] [int] NOT NULL,
    [PlanetName] [varchar](50) NULL,
    [PlanetType] [varchar](50) NULL,
    [Radius] [varchar](50) NULL,
    [TimeCreated] [datetime] NULL
) ON [PRIMARY]
GO
```

Here, the use of [AdventureWorks] changes the database context to AdventureWorks, and the GO command executes the previous set of commands. The CREATE TABLE [dbo].[Planets]command is used to create the Planets table. IndividualID, PlanetName, PlanetType, Radius, and TimeCreated are the columns within the Planets table. Individual ID cannot be NULL. Int, varchar, and datetime specify the data type, which describes what type of data can be entered into the column. (Data types will be explained in detail in Lesson 2.)

ALTER

The ALTER statement changes an existing object; you can use it to add or remove columns from a table, as shown in the following example:

```
ALTER TABLE Shirt
ADD Price Money;
GO
```

Here, ALTER was used to add a Price column to the Shirt table. If you then wanted to set the prices in this column, you could use the UPDATE statement as follows:

```
UPDATE Shirt SET Price = 13.50 WHERE ProductID = 1;
UPDATE Shirt SET Price = 13.50 WHERE ProductID = 2;
UPDATE Shirt SET Price = 10.00 WHERE ProductID = 3;
UPDATE Shirt SET Price = 12.00 WHERE ProductID = 4;
GO
```

You can also use ALTER to change the definition of a view, stored procedure, trigger, or function. For instance, the following command sequence redefines the view to include the Price column:

```
ALTER VIEW Size AS
SELECT ProductID, ProductName, Price FROM Shirt
WHERE ProductType = 'Size';
GO
SELECT * FROM Size
-- Results:
-- ProductID        ProductName        Price
-- _____     _____       _____
-- 1                Red                13.50
-- 2                Blue               13.50
-- 3                Orange             10.00
-- 4                Black              12.00
```

When working with these statements, be careful that you don't confuse ALTER with UPDATE. Remember, ALTER changes the object definition, but UPDATE changes the data in the table.

DROP

The DROP statement actually removes an object from a database, but if other objects are dependent on the object you are attempting to remove, this statement will fail and an error will be raised. The following example shows how you could use DROP to delete data from the Shirts table, then remove it from the Sizes view, and finally remove the Shirts table from the database. In this example, we also try to drop the Person.Contact table, but, as you will notice, this operation fails because there are other objects that are dependent on the Person. Contact table:

```
DELETE FROM Shirt
Select * FROM Size
-- Results:
    -- ProductID        ProductName        Price
    -- _____     _____       _____
-- (0 row(s) affected)
DROP VIEW Size;
GO
DROP TABLE Person.Contact
-- Results:
-- Msg 3726, Level 16, State 1, Line 1
-- Could not drop object 'Person.Contact' because it is referenced by a
FOREIGN KEY constraint.
```

Remember to not confuse DROP, which removes an object from the database, with DELETE, which deletes data from within a table.

TRUNCATE AND DELETE

Two other DDL statements with which you should be familiar are TRUNCATE and DELETE. The DELETE statement is used to delete rows from a table, but it does not free the space containing the table. In comparison, the SQL TRUNCATE command is used to both delete the rows from a table and free the space containing the table.

If you are deleting data from tables in a large database, use TRUNCATE: it is more efficient. Use DELETE for smaller databases.

Thus, to delete all rows from a table named User, you would enter the following command:

```
DELETE FROM user;
```

Similarly, to delete an employee with the identification number 200 from the User table, you would enter the following command:

```
DELETE FROM employee; DELETE FROM user WHERE id = 200;
```

SYSTEM TABLES

When you want to query system views to verify whether the object(s) you wish to drop are, in fact, in the database tables, you need to know what tables are the most useful. System views belong to the sys schema. Some of these system tables include the following:

- sys.Tables
- sys.Columns
- sys.Databases
- sys.Constraints
- sys.Views
- sys.Procedures
- sys.Indexes
- sys.Triggers
- sys.Objects

All of these view names are self-explanatory. For instance, the sys.Objects view contains a row for every object in the database with key column names of name, object_id, type_desc, type, create_date, and modify_date.

SKILL SUMMARY

IN THIS LESSON, YOU LEARNED THE FOLLOWING:

- A database (db) is an organized collection of data, typically stored in electronic format. It allows you to input, organize, and retrieve data quickly.
- Microsoft SQL Server uses three types of files to store databases. Primary data files, with an .mdf extension, are the first files created in a database and can contain user-defined objects, such as tables and views, as well as system tables required by SQL Server to keep track of the database.
- If a database gets too large and you run out of room on your first hard disk, you can create secondary data files, with an .ndf extension, on separate physical hard disks to give your database more room.
- The third type of file used by SQL Server is a transaction log file. Transaction log files use an .ldf extension and don't contain any objects such as tables or views.
- To retrieve data within a database, you run a database query. In other words, a query is used to ask for information from the database and data is then returned.
- A database index is a data structure that improves the speed of data retrieval operations on a database table.
- Most users do not access databases directly. Instead, they use a database management system (DBMS) to access them indirectly.

- A flat-type database is simplistic in design. These databases are most commonly used in plain-text formats, and their purpose is to hold one record per line, making access and queries very rapid.
- Tables, used to store data, are two-dimensional objects consisting of rows and columns.
- A hierarchical database is similar to a tree structure (such as a family tree). Each parent table can have multiple children, but each child table can have only one parent.
- A relational database is similar to a hierarchical database in that data is stored in tables and any new information is automatically added to the table without the need to reorganize the table itself. Unlike tables in a hierarchical database, however, a table in a relational database can have multiple parents.
- Databases are often put on database servers so that they can be accessed by multiple users and provide a higher level of performance. One popular database server is Microsoft SQL Server.
- Constraints are limitations or rules placed on a field or column to ensure that data that is considered invalid is not entered.
- SQL Server Management Studio (SSMS) is the primary tool to manage a server and its databases using a graphical interface.
- Data Manipulation Language (DML) is the language element that allows you to use the core statements INSERT, UPDATE, DELETE, and MERGE to manipulate data in any SQL Server tables.
- Data Definition Language (DDL) is a subset of the Transact-SQL language; it deals with creating database objects like tables, constraints, and stored procedures.

■ Knowledge Assessment

Fill in the Blank

Complete the following sentences by writing the correct word or words in the blanks provided.

1. Database objects are divided into two categories: _____ and _____.

2. Tables created using the _____ statement are used to store data.

3. Constraints can define entity relationships between tables on a continual basis. They are also referred to as _____ constraints.

4. In order to use the *views* object to view a data set, you must use the _____ Transact-SQL statement to show data from underlying tables.

5. DDL influences _____, whereas _____ influences actual data stored in tables.

6. The Microsoft database server that hosts relational databases is called _____.

7. The core DDL statements are _____, _____, _____, _____, _____ and _____.

8. The core DML statements are _____, _____, _____, _____, and _____.

9. System views belong to the _____.

10. The foreign key constraint is a(n) _____ identifier.

Multiple Choice

Circle the letter that corresponds to the best answer.

1. Which of the following is not a DDL statement?
   a. CREATE
   b. MERGE
   c. ALTER
   d. DROP

2. Which of the following is not a column constraint?
   a. Default
   b. Check
   c. Range
   d. Unique

3. What are limitations or rules placed on a field or column to ensure that data that is considered invalid is not entered?
   a. Primary key
   b. index
   c. Foreign key
   d. constraint

4. Which of the following is not a DML statement?
   a. REMOVE
   b. INSERT
   c. DELETE
   d. TRUNCATE

5. Select all of the following statements that are true:
   a. Indexes should only be created on columns that are frequently searched.
   b. A self-reference arises when a foreign key constraint references a column in the same table.
   c. A single INSERT statement can be used to add rows to multiple tables.
   d. Multiple primary keys can be added to a table.

6. Which of the following actions is not supported by ALTER?
   a. Adding a new column to a table.
   b. Deleting multiple columns from an existing table.
   c. Modifying the data type of an existing column.
   d. Changing the identity constraint of an existing column.

7. Which of the following is not a constraint?
   a. Null
   b. Unique
   c. Check
   d. Primary

8. What does SQL stand for?
   a. Structured Question Language
   b. Structured Query Language
   c. Strong Question Language
   d. Specific Query Language

9. Which of the following SQL statements is used to extract data from a database?
   a. SELECT
   b. OPEN
   c. EXTRACT
   d. GET

10. Which SQL statement is used to update data in a database?
    a. SAVE
    b. MODIFY
    c. SAVE AS
    d. UPDATE

Competency Assessment

Scenario 1-1: Considering Database Layout

You have just been hired as a database administrator for an international corporation that is a holding company for many other companies. Your first task is to design a new database infrastructure for the corporation. To begin, reflect on your activities over your first few weeks on the job. List at least one database that you have likely used either directly or indirectly and describe how each database is most likely laid out.

Scenario 1-2: Designing a Relational Database

You have been hired to create a relational database to support a car sales business. You need to store information on the business's employees, inventory, and completed sales. You also need to account for the fact that each salesperson receives a different percentage of their sales in commission. What tables and columns would you create in your relational database, and how would you link the tables?

Proficiency Assessment

Scenario 1-3: Using Help from SQL Server 2008

You recently graduated from school and were hired as a junior database administrator. One thing you've learned over your first few months on the job is that you don't have all the answers. Thankfully, Microsoft SQL Server 2008 has an extensive help system and examples. Say you want to display help regarding use of the CREATE statement so that you can create a table. What steps would you use to find that information in SQL Server 2008's help system?

Scenario 1-4: Creating Databases Using the SSMS Graphical Interface

Your company, AdventureWorks, has decided to expand into interstellar travel. They have asked you to create a new database called Planets on the Microsoft SQL server using the SSMS graphical interface. What steps would you complete to create this database?

LESSON 2

Creating Database Objects

OBJECTIVE DOMAIN MATRIX

SKILLS/CONCEPTS	MTA EXAM OBJECTIVE	MTA EXAM OBJECTIVE NUMBER
Defining Data Types	Choose data types.	2.1
Creating and Using Tables	Understand tables and how to create them.	2.2
Creating Views	Create views.	2.3
Creating Stored Procedures	Create stored procedures and functions.	2.4

KEY TERMS

data type

SQL injection

stored procedures

tables

views

You are a database designer for a large importing/exporting business. Your boss has come to you with a request to help update some of the company's old ways of doing business. She explains that the company will no longer take orders via fax—instead, order requests will be received through a Web server or by email. She expects you to design a database to store and process these electronic orders.

■ Defining Data Types

THE BOTTOM LINE

In this section, you will learn what data types are, why they are important, and how they affect storage requirements. When looking at data types, you need to understand what each type is designed to do within a table, as well as how certain types work best for each column, local variable, expression, or parameter. Also, when choosing a data type to fit your requirements, you need to ensure that whatever type you choose provides the most efficient storage and querying schema. In fact, one of the key roles of a database administrator is to ensure that the data within each database is kept uniform by deciding which data type is best suited to the application module currently being worked on.

A *data type* is an attribute that specifies the type of data an object can hold, as well as how many bytes each data type takes up. For example, several data types handle only whole numbers, which makes them good for counting or for identification. Other data types allow decimal numbers and therefore come in handy when storing values dealing with money. Still other data types are designed to store strings or multiple characters so that you can define labels, descriptions, and comments. Last are other miscellaneous data types that can store dates, times, binary numbers consisting of 0s and 1s, and pictures. As a general rule, if you have two data types that are similar and differ only in how many bytes each uses, one of the data types will have a larger range of values and/or offer increased precision.

Using Built-in Data Types

> Microsoft SQL Server includes a wide range of predefined data types called built-in data types. Most of the databases you will create or use employ only these types of data.

Microsoft SQL Server 2008's built-in data types are organized into the following general categories:

- Exact numbers
- Approximate numbers
- Date and time
- Character strings
- Unicode character strings
- Binary strings
- Other data types
- CLR data types
- Spatial data types

You'll use some of these built-in data types on a regular basis and others more sporadically. Either way, it's important to understand what these data types are and how they are utilized inside a database. Tables 2-1 and 2-2 show the most commonly used data types. Note that in Table 2-2, the asterisk (*) denotes the newest data-type additions in SQL Server 2008.

CERTIFICATION READY
What data type would you use for the cost of an automobile? What type would you use to count the number of cars you have in stock?
2.1

Table 2-1

Most commonly used data types

Data Type	Explanation
Money (numeric)	This numeric data type is used in places where you want money or currency involved in your database; however, if you need to calculate any percentage columns, it is best to use the "float" data type instead. Essentially, the difference between a numeric data type and a float data type rests in whether you are using the data type for approximate numbers or fixed precision. A money or numeric data type is a fixed-precision data type because it must be represented with precision and scale.
Datetime	The datetime data type is used to store date and time data in many different formats. Two main subtypes of this data type—datetime and datetime2—are available, and you should consider what you are using the stored data for when deciding which subtype to use. In particular, if you will be storing values

(continued)

Table 2-1 (*continued*)

DATA TYPE	EXPLANATION
	between the dates of January 1, 1753, and December 31, 9999, that are accurate to 3.33 milliseconds, you should use the datetime data type. In contrast, if you will be storing values between January 1, 1900, and June 6, 2079, that are accurate to only 1 minute, then datetime2 is the data type to use. The second important difference between the two data types is that the datetime data type uses 8 bytes of storage, whereas datetime2 only requires 4 bytes.
Integer	The integer (int) numeric data type is used to store mathematical computations and is employed when you do not require a decimal point output. Examples of integers include the numbers 2 and -2.
Varchar	This character-string data type is commonly used in databases where you are supporting English attributes. If you are supporting multiple languages, use the nvarchar data type instead, as this will help minimize issues of character conversion.
Boolean	The Boolean data type is also known as the bit data type. Here, if your columns store 8 bits or fewer, the columns will be stored as 1 byte; if, they contain 9 to 16 bits, the columns will be stored as 2 bytes; and so forth. The Boolean data type converts true and false string values to bit values, with true converted to 1 and false converted to 0.
Float	The float numeric data type is commonly used in the scientific community and considered an approximate-number data type. This means that not all values within the data-type range will be represented exactly. In addition, depending on which type of float is used, a 4-byte float supports precision up to 7 digits and an 8-byte float supports precision up to 15 digits.

Table 2-2

Data types

DATA TYPE	USE/DESCRIPTION	STORAGE
Exact Numerics:		
bit	Integer with either a 1 or 0 value. (Columns of 9 to 16 bits are stored as 2 bytes, and storage size continues to increase as the number of bits in a column increases.)	1 byte
tinyint	Integer data from 0 to 255.	1 byte
smallint	Integer data from $-2\char94 15$ ($-32,768$) to $2\char94 15-1$ (32,767).	2 bytes
int	Integer data from $-2\char94 31$($-2,147,483,648$) to $2\char94 31-1$ (2,147,483,647).	4 bytes
bigint	Integer data from $-2\char94 63$ ($-9,223,372,036,854,775,808$) to $2\char94 63-1$ (9,223,372,036,854,775,807).	8 bytes
numeric	Fixed precision and scale. Valid values range from $-10\char94 38+1$ through $10\char94 38-1$.	Varies
decimal	Fixed precision and scale. Valid values range from $-10\char94 38+1$ through $10\char94 38-1$.	Varies
smallmoney	Monetary or currency values from $-214,748.3648$ to 214,748.3647.	4 bytes
money	Monetary or currency values from $-922,337,203,685,477.508$ to 922,337, 203,685,477.5807.	8 bytes

Table 2-2 (*continued*)

Data Type	Use/Description	Storage
Approximate Numerics:		
datetime	Defines a date that is combined with a time of day with fractional seconds based on a 24-hour clock. Range: January 1, 1753, through December 31, 9999. Accuracy: Rounded to increments of .000, .003, or .007 seconds.	8 bytes
smalldatetime	Defines a date that is combined with a time of day. The time is based on a 24-hour day, with seconds always zero (:00), meaning there are no fractional seconds. Range: 1900-01-01 through 2079-06-06 (January 1, 1900, through June 6, 2079). Accuracy: one minute.	4 bytes
date*	Defines a date. Range: 0001-01-01 through 9999-12-31. (January 1, 1 AD, through December 31, 9999). Accuracy: one day.	3 bytes
time*	Defines a time of day. This time is without time-zone awareness and is based on a 24-hour clock. Range: 00:00:00.0000000 through 23:59:59.9999999. Accuracy: 100 nanoseconds.	5 bytes
datetimeoffset*	Defines a date that is combined with a time of day that has time-zone awareness and is based on a 24-hour clock. Range: 0001-01-01 through 9999-12-31 (January 1, 1 AD, through December 31, 9999). Range: 00:00:00 through 23:59:59.9999999. Accuracy: 100 nanoseconds.	10 bytes
datetime2*	Defines a date that is combined with a time of day that is based on a 24-hour clock. Range: 0001-01-01 through 999-12-31 (January 1, 1 AD, through December 31, 9999). Range: 00:00:00 through 23:59:59.9999999. Accuracy: 100 nanoseconds.	Varies
Character Strings:		
char	Character data type with fixed length.	Varies
varchar	Character data type with variable length.	Varies
text	This data type will be removed in future SQL releases; therefore, use varchar(max) instead.	Varies
Unicode Character Strings:		
nchar	Character data type with fixed length.	Varies
nvarchar	Character data type with variable length.	Varies
ntext	This data type will be removed in future SQL releases; therefore, use nvarchar(max) instead.	Varies
Binary Strings:		
binary	Binary data with fixed length.	Varies
varbinary	Binary data with variable length.	Varies
image	This data type will be removed in future SQL releases; therefore, use varbinary(max) instead.	Varies
Other Data Types:		
sql_variant	Stores values of various SQL Server-supported data types, except text, ntext, image, timestamp, and sql_variant.	Varies
uniqueidentifier (UUID)	16-byte GUID.	16 bytes

Remember that in SQL Server, each column, local variable, expression, and parameter always has a related data type that defines the storage characteristics of the data being stored. This is shown in Table 2-1.

Now that you have some understanding of the many data types available in Microsoft SQL Server, keep in mind that when two expressions have different data types, collation, precision, scale, or length, the characteristics of the results will be determined as follows:

- When two expressions (mathematical functions or comparison functions) have different data types, rules for data-type precedence specify that the data type with lower precedence is converted to the data type with higher precedence.

- Collation refers to a set of rules that determine how data is sorted and compared. By default, SQL Server has predefined collation precedence. If you wish to override how data is being sorted, you must use a collation clause.

- The precision, scale, and length of the result depend on the precision of the same in the input expression. In other words, if you take several different values and perform a mathematical operation on those values, the precision, scale, and length will be based on those values on which you are performing the mathematical operations.

Now, let's go through some of the most common built-in data types in greater detail so that you are more familiar with how to use them.

Using Exact Numeric Data Types

Exact numeric data types are the most common SQL Server data types used to store numeric information. Some of these data types allow only whole numbers, whereas others allow decimal numbers.

Exact numerics include (but are not limited to) `int`, `bigint`, `bit`, `decimal`, `numeric`, `money`, and `smallmoney`:

- `int` is the primary integer (whole number) data type.
- `bigint` is intended for use when integer values will exceed the `int` data type's range of support. Functions return `bigint` only if the original expression is a `bigint` data type. Note that SQL Server will not automatically promote other integer data types (i.e., `tinyint`, `smallint`, and `int`) to `bigint`.
- `bit` is a Transact-SQL integer data type that takes a value of 1, 0, or NULL and produces the following characteristics:
  - SQL Server Database Engine will optimize the storage of bit columns, meaning that if your table has columns that are 8 or fewer bits wide, these columns will be stored as 1 byte, and if it has 9- to 16-bit columns, they will be stored as 2 bytes. It is important to realize that 1 byte equals 8 bits when considering data types.
  - TRUE and FALSE string values can be converted to bit values. Specifically, TRUE is converted to 1 and FALSE is converted to 0.
- `decimal` and `numeric` are also Transact-SQL data types that have a fixed precision and scale. The syntax for these data types is expressed as follows:

  `decimal[(p[,s])]`

  `numeric[(p[,s])]`

  - `Precision (p)` is the maximum total number of decimal digits that can be stored, both to the left and the right of the decimal point. This value must be a minimum of 1 and a maximum of 38. The default precision number is 18.
  - `Scale(s)` reflects the maximum number of decimal digits that can be stored to the right of the decimal point. This must be a value from 0 through p, but it can be specified only if precision is also specified. The default scale is 0.

- money and smallmoney are Transact-SQL data types you would use to represent monetary or currency values. Both data types are accurate to $1/10,000^{th}$ of the monetary units they represent.

Using Approximate Numeric Data Types

> Approximate numeric data types are not used as often as other SQL Server data types. However, if you need more precision (more decimal places) than is available with the exact numeric data types, you can use either float or real, although you should be aware that these data types typically require additional bytes of storage.

float and real are used in conjunction with floating-point numeric data. This means that all floating data is approximate; thus, not all values that are represented by an approximate data-type range can be expressed accurately.

The syntax of real is float(n). n is the number of bits used to store the mantissa of the float number as represented in scientific notation; therefore, the precision and storage size are dictated if n is actually specified. The value of n must be between 1 and 53, with the default value being 53. The mantissa is the whole number and decimal part of a value but not including place holders and exponents. For example, if you have 3.42732, 3.42732 is the mantissa. But if you have 3.23×10^5, the value is equivalent to 323,000, the mantissa is 3.23.

USING DATE AND TIME DATA TYPES

The date and time data types, of course, deal with dates and times. These data types include date, datetime, datetime2, datetimeoffset, smalldatetime, and time.

date is used to define a date starting with January 1, 1 AD, and ranging to December 31, 9999 AD. Like any data type, the date data type has the descriptors shown in Table 2-3. Although dates themselves are not affected by daylight saving time, you may use dates to determine whether the time on a certain day reflects daylight saving time.

While some of the information in Table 2-3 is self-explanatory, some of it is not. For example, the default string literal format means that by default, it will store the date with the year, followed by the month (two digits), and the day (two digits). It can store any day from January 1, 1 AD to December 31, 9999. The character length means that to display the date, it would take 10 characters such as 2012-03-17. The precision scale shows that it 10 whole numbers with no decimal numbers allowed. To store the date field takes 3 bytes of data. In addition, it is only accurate to one day. So you cannot use decimal number or fractions when dealing with the date value. The default value is 1900-01-01, which means if nothing is defined, it will automatically be assigned January 1, 1900. It uses the Gregorian calendar. Last, it does not use daylight savings time.

Table 2-3

Date descriptions

PROPERTY	VALUE
Syntax	Date
Usage	DECLARE @MyDate date
	CREATE TABLE Table1 (Column1 date)
Default string literal format (used for down-level client)	YYYY-MM-DD (This can be utilized for backward compatibility with down-level clients)
Range	0001-01-01 through 9999-12-31 January 1, 1 AD, through December 31, 9999 AD

(continued)

Table 2-3 (continued)

PROPERTY	VALUE
Element ranges	YYYY is four digits from 0001 to 9999 to represent a year MM is two digits from 01 to 12 to represent a month in a specified year DD is two digits from 01 to 31, depending on the month, that represent a day of the specified month
Character length	10 positions
Precision, scale	10, 0
Storage size	3 bytes, fixed
Accuracy	One day
Default value	1900-01-01 This value is used for the attached date part for inherent conversion from time to datetime2 or datetimeoffset
Calendar	Gregorian
User-defined fractional second precision	No
Time-zone offset aware and preservation	No
Daylight-saving aware	No

In comparison, datetime defines a date that is combined with a time of day expressed with fractional seconds and based on a 24-hour clock. This data type is accurate to 0.00333 seconds. If you need more accuracy, you should use the datetime2 data type, which that is accurate up to 100 nanoseconds. If, however, you don't need to keep track of seconds (which, of course, is less accurate), you can save some storage space by employing the smalldatetime data type instead.

The DateTimeOffset data type is similar to the DateTime data type, but it also keeps track of time zones. For example, if you use two DateTimeOffset values with the same Coordinated Universal Time UTC (which is Greenwich Mean Time in most cases) time in different time zones, the two values will be the same.

If you want to create a data set in which the time of day has time-zone awareness and is based on a 24-hour clock, you will need to use datetimeoffset.

smalldatetime combines a date with a time of day, with the time based on a 24-hour day and with seconds always showing zero as (:00)—meaning that fractional seconds are not provided.

Finally, time defines the time of day based on a 24-hour clock and is without time-zone awareness.

UNDERSTANDING IMPLICIT CONVERSIONS

When working with SQL data, you may wish to convert values from one data type to another. In most situations, these conversions are done automatically. When a conversion is done automatically, it is called an implicit conversion. For example, if you multiply an item's cost (represented as a float) with the number of items (represented as an integer), the answer will be expressed as a float. Figure 2-1 courtesy of Microsoft, provides an in-depth analysis of implicit conversion between data types.

However, some implicit conversions are not allowed. For example, although a DateTime value is represented as a float, you may not implicitly convert DateTime to a float because it

TAKE NOTE*

Use the time, date, datetime2, and dateoffset data types for new work because they align with the SQL standard and are more portable. All but date will provide the most precision for nanosecond applications.

is meant to be a date and/or time. If you have a reason to force a conversion, you can use the Cast and Convert functions.

Cast and Convert offer similar functionality. However, Cast is compliance with ANSI standards, which allow you to import or export to other database management systems. Convert is specific to T-SQL, but is a little bit more powerful.

The syntax of the cast function is:

```
cast(source-value AS destination-type)
```

Therefore, to convert the count variable to a float, you would use the following command:

```
cast(count AS float)
```

The syntax of the convert function is:

```
CONVERT ( data_type [ ( length ) ], expression [,style ] )
```

where you can specify how many digits or characters the value will be. For example:

```
CONVERT(nvarchar(10), OrderDate, 101)
```

This will convert the OrderDate, which is a DateTime data type to nvarchar value. The 101 style represents USA date with century. mm/dd/yyyy.

Figure 2-1

Implicit and explicit conversion types

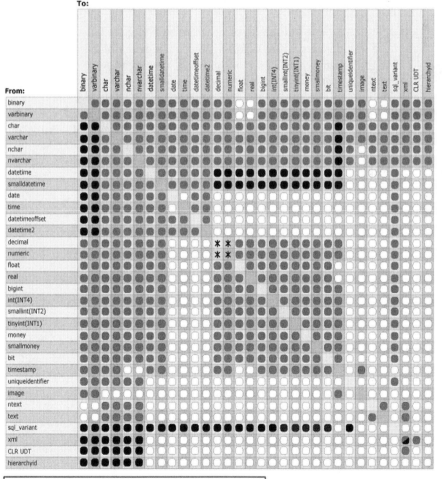

USING CHARACTER STRINGS

A regular character uses one byte of storage for each character, which allows you to define one of 256 (8 bits are in a byte, and 2^8 = 256) possible characters, accommodating English and some European languages. A Unicode character uses two bytes of storage per character so that you can represent one of 65,536 (16 bits are in 2 bytes, and 2^16 = 65,536) characters. The additional space allows Unicode to store characters from just about any language, including Chinese, Japanese, Arabic, and so on.

As you write the syntax for the different data types, remember that they also differ in the way literals (fixed data value) are expressed. A regular character literal is always expressed with single quotes. For example:

`'This is how a regular character string literal looks'`

However, when you are expressing a Unicode character literal, it must have the letter N (for National) prefixing the single quote. For example:

`N'This is how a Unicode character string literal looks'`

When you use a VAR element, SQL Server will preserve space in the row in which that element resides based on the column's defined size (and not on the actual number of characters in the character string itself), plus an extra two bytes of data for offset data. For example, if you want to specify that a string supports a maximum of only 25 characters, you would use VARCHAR(25).

Storage consumption, when using Unicode data types, is reduced from that of the regular data type, thus allowing faster read operations; however, the price you pay for using this data type is in the possibility of row expansion, leading to data movement outside the current page. This means that any update of data using variable-length data types may be less efficient than updates using fixed-length data types. It is possible to define the variable-length data type with the MAX specifier, however, instead of using the maximum number of characters identified in the string. For example, when a column is defined with the MAX specifier, a value with a size identified up to a certain threshold (the default is 8,000) is stored inline in the row. Then, should you specify a value with a size greater than the default threshold, that value will be stored external to the row and identified as a large object, or LOB.

These are the most widely used character data types and are either of a fixed or variable length. Each has its own individual characteristics that you need to take into consideration when deciding which will have a positive effect on storage requirements. Both char and varchar data sets need to be defined, or assigned, within the data definition, or they may affect the maximum storage limits.

The data set char is identified as char [(n)] and is a fixed-length, non-Unicode character (in other words, regular character) with a length of n bytes. The value of n must be between 1 and 8,000, making the storage size n bytes. The other non-Unicode data type, varchar[(n|max)], is a variable-length data set that can consist of 1 to 8,000 characters.

Microsoft SQL Server supports only two character string types: regular and Unicode. Regular data types include those identified with CHAR and VARCHAR. Unicode data types are identified with NCHAR and NVARCHAR. Simple? Yes, in the sense that the differences between regular and Unicode are the bytes of storage used for each.

The Unicode character strings `nchar` and `nvarchar` can either be fixed or variable, like the regular character strings; however, these strings use the UNICODE UCS-2 character set.

Creating and Using Tables

THE BOTTOM LINE

In this section, you will develop an understanding of the purpose of tables. You'll also explore how to create tables in a database using proper ANSI SQL syntax.

The purpose of a ***table*** is to provide a structure for storing data within a relational database. Without this structure, there is an increased probability of database failure. In Lesson 1, you learned about the purposes of tables and how to create them. Let's quickly review some of the most important points to remember when creating a table in a nongraphical user interface. As we do so, be sure to think about the purpose of a relational database in the hierarchy of database administration.

A SQL database is the central container that retrieves data from many different tables and views. You can run queries on these data, thereby interacting with the information stored in the database to obtain the output you require. One advantage of a database over a series of spreadsheets is that a database can parse out redundant storage and information obtained from various relational spreadsheets.

As in programming, when you are designing, creating, and using databases, you can easily use hundreds of objects, including databases, tables, columns, views, and stored procedures. Therefore, to make your company's database easier to manage, your organization should establish and use a single, consistent standard. Of course, this also means documenting this standard and distributing it to everyone who works with the database.

It really doesn't make any difference how you use uppercase and lowercase in a database, as long as you are consistent. Two common naming conventions are PascalCase and camelCase. Examples of PascalCase are such names as OrderDetails or CustomerAddresses, whereas examples of camelCase are names like myAddress and vendorTerms. No matter which standard you use, you should always be sure to use names that are both accurate and descriptive. You should also avoid using spaces because they add complications that make it necessary for you to use quotes. Instead, use underscores (_) as word separators or use mixed upper and lower case characters.

Let's first learn how to create a new table using SQL Server Management Studio (SSMS) before we move on to the syntax method of table creation.

 CREATE A TABLE USING SSMS

GET READY. Before you begin, be sure to launch SQL Server Management Studio. Make sure you've expanded the particular database in which you wish to create the new table, then follow these steps:

1. Right-click the **Table** folder and select **New Table**, as shown in Figure 2-2:

Figure 2-2

Creating a new table

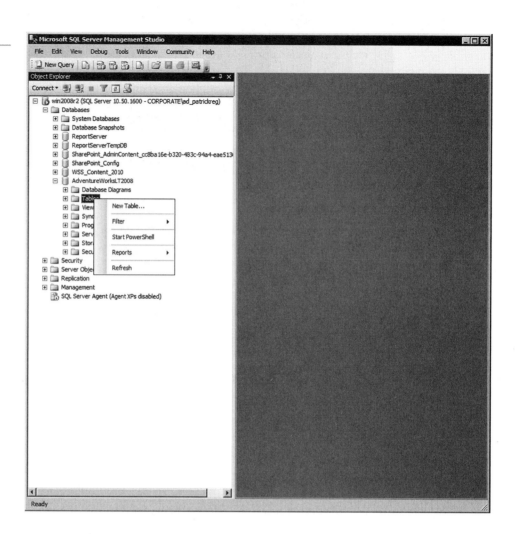

2. Use the information shown in Figure 2-3 to complete the details for Column Name, Data Type, and Length, as specified in the parentheses and Allow Nulls columns.

Figure 2-3

Column names and identifying information

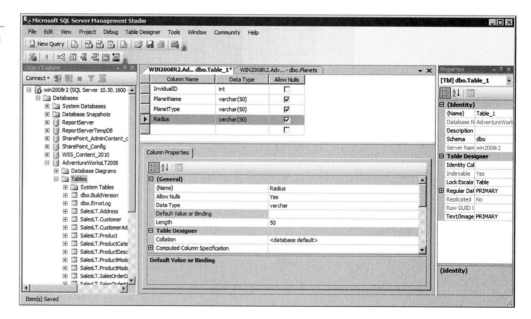

3. Set the Default Value of the DateCreated column to *(getdate())*; this will insert the current date within each new record for that specific field. See Figure 2-4.

Figure 2-4

Setting the Table Designer properties

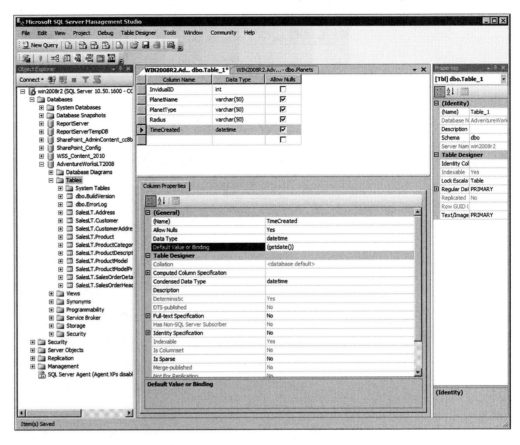

4. Save your new table by selecting File > Save Table_1, as shown in Figure 2-5.

Figure 2-5

Saving the new table

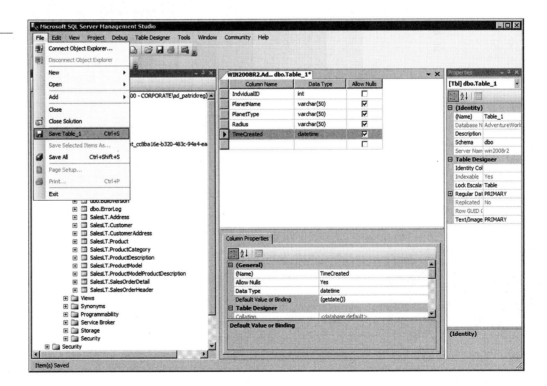

5. Type the new name of the table you are saving, as shown in Figure 2-6.

Figure 2-6

Naming the table

Your new table will appear under the **Tables** section, as depicted in Figure 2-7.

Figure 2-7

The newly created table

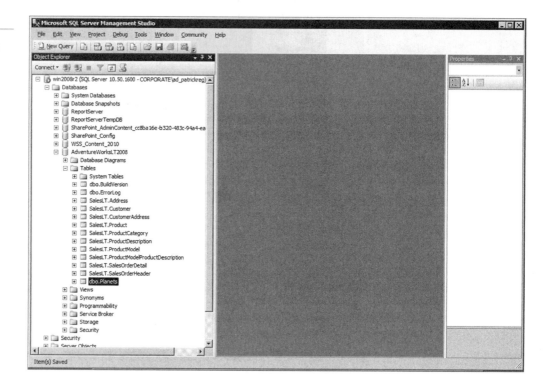

PAUSE. Leave the SSMS interface open for the next exercise.

 CREATE A TABLE USING TRANSACT-SQL COMMANDS

Creating tables within SSMS is simple because SSMS is an easy-to-use graphical interface. But how can you create tables using ANSI SQL syntax? Quite simply, you will use the `create table` statement to accomplish this task. An example of proper Transact-SQL syntax for creating a table is as follows:

```
CREATE TABLE planets (name varchar(50), diameter varchar(50))
INSERT INTO planets (name, diameter) VALUES ('earth', 10000)
```

Note that if SQL Server didn't support implicit conversion, the following syntax would be needed:

```
CREATE TABLE planets (name varchar(50), diameter varchar(50))
INSERT INTO planets (name, diameter) VALUES ('earth', CAST (10000 as varchar(50)))
```

■ Creating Views

As a database administrator, you must understand when to use views. You should also know how to create views by using either a Transact-SQL statement or the graphical designer.

A *view* is simply a virtual table consisting of different columns from one or more tables. Unlike a table, a view is stored in a database as a query object; therefore, a view is an object that obtains its data from one or more tables. Views that are based on this definition are referred to as underlying tables. Once you have defined a view, you can reference it as you would any other table in a database.

A view is meant to be a security mechanism; that is, a view ensures that users can retrieve and modify only the data seen by them through their permissions, thus ensuring they cannot see or access the remaining data in the underlying tables. A view is also a mechanism to simplify query execution. Complex queries can be stored in the form of a view and data from the view can then be mined using simple query statements.

Views ensure the security of data by restricting access to the following data:

- Specific rows of tables
- Specific columns of tables
- Specific rows and columns of tables
- Rows obtained by using joins
- Statistical summaries of data in given tables
- Subsets of another view or subsets of views and tables

Some common examples of views include the following:

- A subset of rows or columns of a base table
- A union of two or more tables
- A join of two or more tables
- A statistical summary of base tables
- A subset of another view or some combination of views and base tables

Database views are designed to create a virtual table that is representative of one or more tables in an alternative way. There are two major reasons you might want to provide a view instead of enabling users to access the underlying tables in your database:

- Views allow you to limit the type of data users can access. You can grant view permissions in designated tables, and you can also choose to deny permissions for certain information.
- Views reduce complexity for end users so they don't have to learn how to write complex SQL queries. Instead, you can write those queries on their behalf and hide them in a view.

When creating a view, be sure to consider database performance in your design. As discussed briefly in Lesson 1, indexing plays a role in query time and an even greater role in database performance improvements. But tread lightly: Adding indexes to the schema can actually increase the overhead of your database due to the ongoing maintenance of these indexes.

There are two methods for creating a view:

- By using SSMS
- By writing a Transact-SQL statement

We'll cover both procedures in this section.

CREATE A VIEW USING SSMS

GET READY. Before you begin these steps, make sure SSMS is open and the database to which you wish to add a view is highlighted. Then, follow these steps to create your view:

1. Expand the Views section by clicking the plus sign (+) next to Views.

   Right-click the Views folder as shown in Figure 2-8, then select New View.

Figure 2-8

Creating a new view

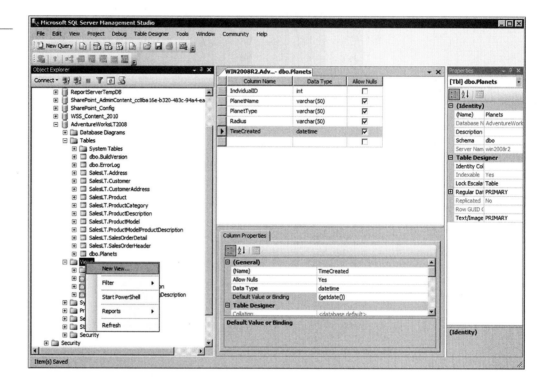

The Add Table dialog box will open (see Figure 2-9).

Figure 2-9

Add Table dialog box

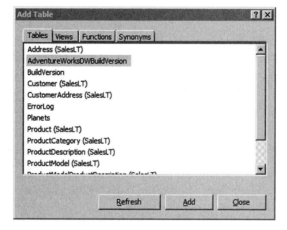

Let's explain a little bit about what this dialog box allows you to do:

- To specify the table to be used as the primary source, click the appropriate table in the Tables tab of the dialog box.
- To use another existing view, click the Views tab of the dialog box.

- If you want to generate records from a function, you will find that on the Functions tab.
- If you want to use more than one source, you can click each of the different tabs to find the table, view, or function you wish to add to your query.
- Once you have selected the desired source(s), simply click the Add button for each one.
- Once you have selected and added all your desired sources, click the Close button to exit the Add Table dialog box.

2. As you click Add to add each source, you will see the information shown in Figure 2-10.

Figure 2-10

Add Table dialog box output

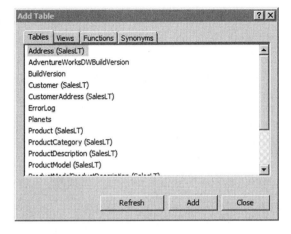

After you have selected the objects you wish to use, the View Designer toolbar will be added, in which you can further map out the views you wish to incorporate into your query.

CERTIFICATION READY
How do you create a
view using SSMS?
2.3

You can also create views using Transact-SQL. Here, once you add your sources to the diagram pane, the syntax for these sources is shown in the SQL pane.

To create a view using Transact-SQL syntax, a simple convention is as follows:

```
CREATE VIEW vwCustomer

AS

SELECT CustomerId, Company Name, Phone

      FROM Customers
```

This creates a view called vwCustomer that will be stored as an object. Here, the data that is queried from the columns comes from the Customers table.

■ Creating Stored Procedures

↓
THE BOTTOM LINE

By creating stored procedures and functions, you make it possible to select, insert, update, or delete data using these statements.

So far, you've learned how to use different data types to create tables and views through the SSMS interface as well as through Transact-SQL syntax statements. Now it's time to learn how to create stored procedure statements using the same graphic interface.

A *stored procedure* is a previously written SQL statement that has been "stored" or saved into a database. One way to save time when running the same query over and over again is to create a stored procedure that you can then execute from within the database's command environment. An example of executing a stored procedure is as follows:

```
exec usp_displayallusers
```

Here, the name of the stored procedure is "usp_displayallusers," and "exec" tells SQL Server to execute the code in the stored procedure. Indeed, when you create your own stored procedure, it will have the designation "usp" in front of it, which indicates to SQL that this is a user-created stored procedure.

Now, say that your stored procedure named "displayallusers" has a simple code inside it, such as the following:

```
SELECT * FROM USERLIST
```

What this select statement does is return all the data that is found in the USERLIST table. One question you may be asking right now is, "Why can't I just run the query I want to return the information I need? In other words, you may wonder why you should bother with creating a stored procedure. Note that the "*" you see in the above statement means you are not defining criteria you would like matched in the output. In other words, you are returning *all* records from the userlist table.

Perhaps you are working on a website built with ASP pages and you need to call a stored procedure from that, or from within another application such as Visual Basic, or from another application entirely. Using a stored procedure allows you to store all the logic inside the database, so by using a simple command, you can query and retrieve all information from all sources.

A stored procedure is an already-written SQL statement that is stored in a database. If you are continually using the same SQL statement within your database, it is simpler to create a stored procedure for it. Now, simple statements like a "select" statement would not entirely benefit from a stored procedure, but if you are creating complex query statements, your best bet is to create a stored procedure for them and run that stored procedure from within the Query Analyzer using an execute (exec) command.

 CREATE A STORED PROCEDURE

GET READY. Before you begin these steps, make sure SSMS is open and the database to which you wish to add a view is highlighted. Then, follow these steps to create a stored procedure:

1. Expand the Programmability section by clicking the appropriate + sign, then expand the Stored Procedure section by clicking the appropriate + sign.

2. Right-click Stored Procedures and choose New Stored Procedure (see Figure 2-11).

Figure 2-11

New Stored Procedure selection menu

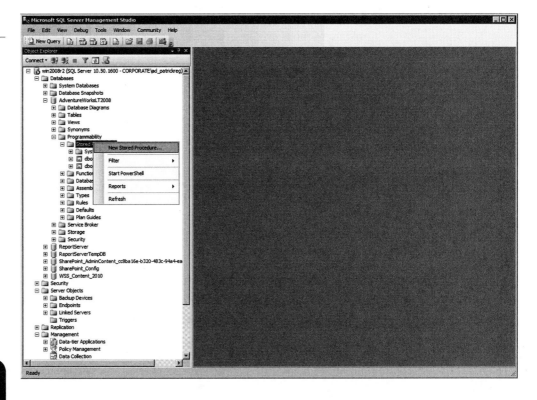

CERTIFICATION READY
How would you create a stored procedure with SSMS?
2.4

The Text Editor window will open (see Figure 2-12), displaying the syntax. The window contains a ready-made stored procedure template for you to add your own view parameters.

Figure 2-12

Sample Text Editor window

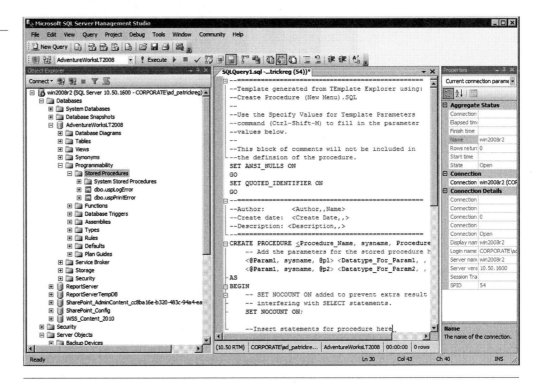

Microsoft SQL Server already has hundreds of system-stored procedures so that you can perform basic functions. For example, you can use the Select Stored Procedure to retrieve or select rows from a database. Some of the more popular stored procedures will be covered in the next lesson including SELECT, INSERT, UPDATE, and DELETE.

Understanding SQL Injections

Before you learn the syntax statements for selecting, inserting, updating, and deleting data, you need to understand what a SQL injection is. In short, a *SQL injection* is an attack in which malicious code is inserted into strings that are later passed on to instances of SQL Server waiting for parsing and execution. Any procedure that constructs SQL statements should be reviewed continually for injection vulnerabilities because SQL Server will execute all syntactically valid queries from any source.

The primary form of SQL injection is a direct insertion of code into user-input variables that are concatenated with SQL commands and then executed. A less direct method of attack injects malicious code into strings that are destined for storage in a table or are considered metadata. When these stored strings are subsequently concatenated into the dynamic SQL command, the malicious code will be executed.

The injection process's function is to terminate a text string prematurely and append a new command directed from it; because the inserted command may have additional strings appended to it before it is executed, the malefactor terminates the injected string with a comment mark "—", making subsequent text ignored at execution time.

SKILL SUMMARY

IN THIS LESSON, YOU LEARNED THE FOLLOWING:

- A data type is an attribute that specifies the type of data an object can hold, as well as how many bytes each data type takes up.
- As a general rule, if you have two data types that differ only in how many bytes each uses, the one with more bytes has a larger range of values and/or increased precision.
- Microsoft SQL Server includes a wide range of predefined data types called built-in data types. Most of the databases you will create or use will employ only these data types.
- Exact numeric data types are the most common SQL Server data types used to store numeric information.
- int is the primary integer (whole number) data type.
- Precision (p) is the maximum total number of decimal digits that can be stored in a numeric data type, both to the left and to the right of the decimal point; this value must be at least 1 and at most 38. The default precision number is 18.
- money and smallmoney are Transact-SQL data types you would use to represent monetary or currency values. Both data types are accurate to 1/10,000th of the monetary units they represent.
- Approximate numeric data types are not as commonly used as other SQL Server data types. If you need more precision (more decimal places) than is available with the exact numeric data types, you should use the float or real data types, both of which typically take additional bytes of storage.
- The date and time data types, of course, deal with dates and times. These data types include date, datetime2, datetime, datetimeoffset, smalldatetime, and time.

- SQL Server supports implicit conversions, which can occur without specifying the actual callout function (cast or convert). Explicit conversions require you to use the functions cast or convert specifically.

- A regular character uses one byte of storage for each character, which allows you to define one of 256 possible characters; this accommodates English and some European languages.

- A Unicode character uses two bytes of storage per character so that you can represent one of 65,536 characters. This added capacity means that Unicode can store characters from almost any language.

- When you use a VAR element, SQL Server will preserve space in the row in which this element resides on the basis of on the column's defined size and not the actual number of characters in the character string itself.

- The Unicode character strings nchar and nvarchar can either be fixed or variable, like regular character strings; however, they use the UNICODE UCS-2 character set.

- The purpose of a table is to provide a structure for storing data within a relational database.

- A view is simply a virtual table that consists of different columns from one or more tables. Unlike a table, a view is stored in a database as a query object; therefore, a view is an object that obtains its data from one or more tables.

- A stored procedure is a previously written SQL statement that has been stored or saved into a database.

- A SQL injection is an attack in which malicious code is inserted into strings that are later passed on to instances of SQL Server for parsing and execution.

Knowledge Assessment

Fill in the Blank

Complete the following sentences by writing the correct word or words in the blanks provided.

1. Each _____, _____, expression, and _____ always has a related data type.

2. A bit is a Transact-SQL integer data type that can take a _____ of 1, 0, or NULL.

3. When you are defining the cost of a product, it is best to use the _____ data type.

4. It is important to consider your use of _____ data sets when building tables dependent on daylight saving time.

5. SQL Server supports _____ conversions without using actual callout functions (cast or convert).

6. A regular character uses _____ byte(s) of storage for each character, whereas a Unicode character requires _____ byte(s) of storage.

7. The data set char is of _____ length and has a length of _____ bytes.

8. The purpose of a table is to provide a(n) _____ for storing data within a relational database.

9. When creating a view, be sure to consider _____ in your design.

10. When querying a database, you can obtain faster results from properly _____ tables and views.

Multiple Choice

Circle the letter that corresponds to the best answer.

1. Which of the following is not a data type?
   a. Exact numerics
   b. Approximate numerics
   c. ANSI string
   d. Spatial

2. What do you call when a data type is converted automatically to another data type?
   a. `implicit conversion`
   b. `explicit conversion`
   c. `dynamic conversion`
   d. `static conversion`

3. Which of the following is not true about the `int` data type?
   a. int is an integer.
   b. `bigint` is used when the value will exceed `int` data type's range.
   c. An Integer uses 8 bytes to store data.
   d. Functions will return `bigint` only if the original expression has the same data type.

4. Do implicit conversions require an actual callout feature (i.e., `cast` or `convert`)?
   a. Yes
   b. No

5. Select all of the following statements that are false:
   a. A table provides structure to store data.
   b. A database retrieves data from different tables and views.
   c. A database cannot parse out redundant data.
   d. A table can be created both in a graphical interface and by using syntax.

6. Which of the following statements best describes the importance of creating views?
   a. Views give users the ability to access underlying tables.
   b. Views allow you to limit the type of data users can access.
   c. Views reduce the complexity for end users so they don't need to learn complex SQL queries.
   d. Both a and b
   e. Both b and c
   f. All of the above

7. Which of the following statements does not accurately describe a view?
   a. A view is a virtual table.
   b. A view is meant to serve as a security mechanism.
   c. Views should not be used for granting access.
   d. A view simplifies query execution.

8. What is the Transact-SQL statement to create a view?
   a. `CREATE VIEW`
   b. `CREATE VIEW view_name`
   c. `CREATE VIEW view_name *`

9. Which statement is used to suppress the '(1 row(s) affected)' after executing query statements?
   a. `SET NO COUNT`
   b. `SET NOCOUNT ON`
   c. `SET NO COUNTING`
   d. `SET NO COUNTING ON`

10. Which is not a regular data type?
    a. CHAR
    b. NCHAR
    c. TEXT
    d. VARCHAR

Competency Assessment

Scenario 2-1: Calculating the Size of a Table

As a new database administrator, you have been asked to create a large employee database that will store information for 10,000 employees.

You have the following columns defined in the table:

FirstName	varchar(50)
LastName	varchar(50)
StreetAddress	varchar(75)
State	varchar(2)
ZipCode	varchar(9)
Age	int
BirthDate	date

How many bytes would you need to store each record? How many bytes would you use to store 10,000 records?

Scenario 2-2: Choosing Data Types

You are designing several databases for a client. While designing the databases, you come across the following listed data items. Which data type would you use to store each of these pieces of information and why?

Radius of a planet

Value of pi (π)

Salary

Person's date of birth

Length of a board

Numbers of music players sold

Proficiency Assessment

Scenario 2-3: Understanding Tables and How to Create Them

You have been hired as a new database administrator and told to create a customer database. After opening SSMS and accessing the AdventureWorks database, what query command would you use to create a table called customers.customer with the following columns or fields?

Unique Customer ID

CompanyID—Up to 50 characters

FirstName—Up to 50 characters

LastName—Up to 50 characters

ModifiedDate

Scenario 2-4: Extracting Data from a Database

You are a database administrator for the AdventureWorks Corporation, and a service manager needs your help extracting data from the company's database. Therefore, after opening SSMS and accessing the AdventureWorks database, specify the basic SELECT statements you would use to retrieve the required information from the ProductsSubcategory table.

1. What commands would return all the rows and columns in the ProductCategory table?

2. What commands would you type and execute to return only the *ProductSubcategoryID*, *ProductCategoryID*, *Name*, and *ModifiedDate* columns?

3. What commands would you type and execute to return rows where the word *bike* appears somewhere in the *Name* column?

4. In the existing query window, what commands would you use to add a column alias to the *Name* column to clarify it as the subcategory name?

5. In the existing query window, what command would you use to sort the previous result set?

Manipulating Data

OBJECTIVE DOMAIN MATRIX

SKILLS/CONCEPTS	MTA EXAM OBJECTIVE	MTA EXAM OBJECTIVE NUMBER
Using Queries to Select Data	Select data.	3.1
Using Queries to Insert Data	Insert data.	3.2
Updating Data and Databases	Update data.	3.3
Deleting Data	Delete data.	3.4

KEY TERMS

cross join

delete

intersect

join

referential integrity

select

transactions

union

update

You have just been hired by a medium-sized company and asked to provide employee record lists to the newly hired vice president of Human Resources. In order to manipulate the data to fit the vice president's needs, you must create a variety of different lists using Transact-SQL statements.

Although the title of this lesson refers to manipulating data for query purposes, it's important to note that querying is itself considered a form of data modification because it involves changing query statements to obtain a desired output. No matter the name or descriptor, the object of any database is for the user to be able to extract data from it. In fact, the vast majority of SQL statements are designed to retrieve user-requested information from a database through the use of queries. In this lesson, we'll look at some of the most important query statements you must understand to further your understanding of Transact-SQL.

■ Using Queries to Select Data

THE BOTTOM LINE

In this section, you'll learn how to utilize the SELECT query to retrieve or extract data from a table, how to retrieve or extract data using joins, and how to combine results using UNION and INTERSECT.

The SQL command for retrieving any data from a database is SELECT. Much like any other SQL command, SELECT is similar to an English statement. Composing a SELECT statement is akin to filling in the blanks, as shown in the following example:

```
SELECT id, name //columns
FROM sysobjects // tables
WHERE type = "jones" //conditions you wish to produce results from
```

This simple example provides a basic understanding of what the SELECT statement does. You will always follow the same pattern each time you issue a SELECT statement to a database. Moreover, there are only three things you need to be sure to identify in your statement to form a proper SELECT query:

- Columns to retrieve
- Tables to retrieve the columns from
- Conditions, if any, that the data must satisfy

The previous constructs are considered your framework for creating SELECT query statements using the SQL text editor window. Let's say, for example, that you want to give your boss a list of employees whose salary is above $50,000 per year. You are interested in retrieving only those employees who fit that criteria. Here's how you could do this in SQL:

```
SELECT first_name, last_name, salary
FROM employees
WHERE salary >= 50,000
```

This query would then produce the following results:

first_name	last_name	salary
John	Allan	52,000
Sylvia	Goddard	51,200
Julia	Smith	55,000
David	Thompson	62,900

(4 row(s) affected)

If you want to select only a single column for your query, you can identify the name of the column by typing it between *select* and *from* in the query statement. To identify more than one column to include in your query (as in the above example), simply type each column name and separate the names with a comma. The reason for using a comma instead of a space is that SQL treats a space as an identifier, or match word, such as "value" or "select." Thus, if you need to use a space in your statement, you need to enclose the words in square brackets or double quotes—for example, [select] or "value."

If you wish to choose all columns from within a table, you can do so by typing an asterisk (*) in the place where the column name(s) would otherwise be given.

The only required component of the SQL SELECT query is the SELECT ... FROM clause, meaning that you could select all available fields from one table simply by issuing the following command:

```
SELECT *
FROM employees
```

This could produce a large result or a small result, depending on the number of employees within a company. Let's use an example of a company with only six employees. If we entered the above command, our result would look similar to the following:

first_name	last_name	employee_id	phone	gender
Jim	Alexander	610001	574-555-0001	M
Frances	Drake	610002	574-555-0346	F
David	Thompson	610003	574-555-0985	M
Alexandria	Link	610004	574-555-9087	F
Peter	Link	610005	574-555-7863	M
Antoin	Drake	610006	574-555-2597	M

(6 row(s) affected)

You now have a basic understanding of what the SELECT statement is designed to do. But what if you want to retrieve only specific types of data from the tables you identified with your original SELECT ... FROM query statement? This is when the WHERE clause comes in handy. For instance, the WHERE clause could be added to a query to find only those employees who work in the company's shipping department, as shown here:

```
SELECT first_name, last_name
FROM employees
WHERE department = 'shipping'
```

This would return the following result:

first_name	last_name
Jim	Alexander
Frances	Drake
David	Thompson

(3 row(s) affected)

Combining Conditions

Perhaps you require more from a query than simply one set of parameters. In such cases, you can combine several conditions in one query statement. For instance, in the previous example, we ran a query that returned only those employees who work in the shipping department. Say you now want that result *and* you want to determine which of these employees are female. You could obtain this desired result using the following SQL statement:

```
SELECT first_name, last_name
FROM employees
WHERE department = 'shipping' AND gender = 'F' AND hired >=
'2000-JAN-01'
```

The expected output shows the following results:

```
first_name              last_name
------------            ------------
Frances                 Drake
(1 row(s) affected)
```

Thus, this query uses the AND conjunction to yield the names of all employees who are in the shipping department *and* who are female.

You can also use the OR conjunction to return a result that meets *either* of two conditions, as shown below:

```
SELECT first_name, last_name
FROM employees
WHERE department = 'shipping' OR employee_id <= 610007
```

This would return the following result:

```
first_name              last_name
------------            ------------
James                   Alexander
David                   Thompson
Frances                 Drake
Alexandria              Link
Peter                   Link
Antoin                  Drake
(6 row(s) affected)
```

In this example, notice that the query yields not just the three employees in the shipping department (thereby meeting the first condition), but also three new rows of data that satisfy *only* the second condition of the query (i.e., an employee ID number less than 610007). This means that Alexandria Link, Peter Link, and Antoin Drake meet the second condition in the WHERE query statement, but not the first.

Using the BETWEEN Clause

In some situations, you may need to retrieve records that satisfy a range condition and also contain a value within a range of another specified value. For instance, perhaps you need to retrieve a list of employees who were hired between 1990 and 2000. One way you can obtain this result is to join the two conditions using the AND conjunction:

```
SELECT first_name, last_name, hire_date
FROM employees
WHERE hire_date >= '1-Jan-1990' AND hire_date <= '1-Jan-2000'
```

This query would produce the following results:

```
first_name          last_name          hire_date
------------        ------------       ------------
James               Alexander          1990-12-10
Frances             Drake              1998-03-04
Peter               Link               1997-07-08
Antoin              Drake              1999-12-31
(4 row(s) affected)
```

You may be wondering what this query is really doing based on the two conditions and why the syntax looks awkward. To help resolve the awkwardness in the AND clause in this query statement, try replacing it with a BETWEEN clause. This allows you to specify the range to be used in a "between x and y" query format, yielding a much cleaner statement. Let's rewrite the previous statement to reflect the *between* condition instead:

```
SELECT first_name, last_name, hire_date
FROM employees
WHERE hire_date BETWEEN '1-Jan-1990' AND '1-Jan-2000'
```

With this statement, you will receive exactly the same output as with the previous query statement.

Using the NOT Clause

In some instances, it is simpler to write your query in terms of what you *don't* want in your output. Transact-SQL provides you with the NOT keyword for precisely such situations. For example, say you want a list of all employees who don't work in the shipping department. You could obtain this list using the following query:

```
SELECT first_name, last_name
FROM employees
WHERE NOT department = 'shipping'
```

The use of operators, as shown in this and several earlier examples, can help in achieving the same results in many instances. Thus, you could write a query using a < (greater than) and a > (less than) operator in place of an equal sign. Doing so would yield the following query statement:

```
SELECT first_name, last_name
FROM employees
WHERE department <> 'shipping'
```

No matter which way you write the syntax for the query statement, it will produce the same results.

Using the UNION Clause

The UNION clause allows you to combine the results of two or more queries into a resulting single set that includes all the rows belonging to the query in that union. The UNION clause is entirely different from the JOIN statements, which combine columns from two different tables. You must remember a couple of basic rules when combining the results of two queries via the UNION clause:

- The number and order of the columns must be the same in each of the queries in the clause.
- The data types you use must be compatible.

For instance, you could use the UNION clause as follows to create a query that returns a list of all employees in the shipping department who were hired between January 1, 1990, and January 1, 2000:

```
SELECT first_name, last_name
FROM employees
WHERE department = 'shipping'
UNION
SELECT first_name, last_name
FROM employees
WHERE hire_date BETWEEN '1-Jan-1990' AND '1-Jan-2000'
```

Using the EXCEPT and INTERSECT Clauses

Both the EXCEPT and the INTERSECT statements are designed to return distinct values by comparing the results of two queries. In particular, the EXCEPT clause gives you the final result set where data exists in the first query and not in the second dataset. The INTERSECT gives you the final result set where values in both of the queries match by the query on both the left and right sides of the operand.

The same two basic rules apply to use of the EXCEPT and INTERSECT clauses as apply to use of the UNION clause:

- The number and order of the columns must be the same in all queries.
- The data types must be compatible.

For example, say you worked in a factory setting, and you wanted to retrieve one list showing products with work orders and another list showing products without any work orders. You could structure the query as follows, first using the INTERSECT clause:

```
SELECT ProductID
FROM Production.Product // The database name is Production and
        the table name is Product
INTERSECT
SELECT ProductID
FROM Production.WorkOrder;
--Result: 238 Rows (products that have work orders)
```

Here's the same query, but using the EXCEPT clause:

```
SELECT ProductID
FROM Production.Product
EXCEPT
SELECT ProductID
FROM Production.WorkOrder;
--Result: 266 Rows (products without work orders)
```

Using the JOIN Clause

The JOIN clause allows you to combine related data from multiple table sources. JOIN statements are similar in application to both EXCEPT and INTERSECT in that they return values from two separate table sources. Using this knowledge, let's see what data can be extracted through the use of JOIN statements.

JOIN statements can be specified in either the FROM or the WHERE clause, but it is recommended that you specify them in the FROM clause.

There are three types of JOIN statements you should be aware of:

- Inner joins allow you to match related records taken from different source tables.
- Outer joins can include records from one or both tables you are querying that do not have any corresponding record(s) in the other table. There are three types of outer joins: LEFT OUTER JOIN, RIGHT OUTER JOIN, and FULL OUTER JOIN.
- Cross joins return all rows from one table along with all rows from the other table. WHERE conditions should always be included.

For instance, you could use the most common of the JOIN statements, INNER JOIN, if you wanted to retrieve a list of employees by their ID numbers and match each employee with the ID of his or her current department supervisor. For this type of query, you will have to identify the matching column in each of the tables you wish to write the query against and obtain the desired output from. In this example, the foreign key in Table 3-1 is identified in the column "department_id," and in Table 3-2, the foreign key is identified as the "department" column match: In other words, the Department table's Department ID is linked to the department column in the Employee table

Table 3-1

Employee table

first_name	last_name	employee_id	department
James	Alexander	610001	1
David	Thompson	620002	1
Frances	Drake	610003	1
Alexandria	Link	610004	2
Peter	Link	620005	2
David	Cruze	610007	NULL

Table 3-2

Department table

department_id	first_name	last_name
1	Jane	Horton
2	Mitch	Simmons
3	Paul	Franklin

Trying to combine data between tables can be very cumbersome, especially if you are creating specific lists from thousands of rows of data. Using a SELECT statement query lets you produce individual lists, but the result may be that you get all the information you need but in an individual list format.

The INNER JOIN keyword simplifies this data retrieval by not only using the information from the two tables from which you require output, but using the INNER JOIN keyword to specify the required conditions for which records will appear For example, from the two example tables, you may wish to create a list showing which employees work for each of the different department supervisors. You would write the SQL query statement as follows:

```
SELECT employee.first_name, employee.last_name,
       department.first_name, department.last_name
FROM employee INNER JOIN department
ON employee.department = department.department_id
```

The resulting output is shown below:

first_name	last_name	first_name	last_name
James	Alexander	JaneHorton	
David	Thompson	JaneHorton	
Frances	Drake	JaneHorton	
Alexandria	Link Mitch	Simmons	
Peter	Link Mitch	Simmons	
Antoin	Drake	PaulFranklin	

(6 row(s) affected)

Did you notice that David Cruze does not appear in the output list of employees matched with department supervisors? In the department column, his name is not identified as being in any department, although he is an employee. This could happen for a variety of reasons; perhaps he is a new hire and has not officially started working for any department.

Perhaps your employer would like a list of records from the second table that do not actually match any of your previous conditions. Any of the OUTER JOIN statements, LEFT OUTER JOIN, RIGHT OUTER JOIN, or FULL OUTER JOIN, can yield the query output you desire. The OUTER JOIN statements begin where the results of INNER JOIN finish and include all records in the left table along with the matching records of the right table AND any non-matching records.

A sample LEFT OUTER JOIN statement includes the statement from the INNER JOIN shown previously and also includes the non-matching clause:

```
SELECT employee.first_name, employee.last_name,
       department.first_name, department.last_name
FROM employee LEFT OUTER JOIN department
ON employee.department = department.department_id
```

The resulting output would be as follows:

first_name	last_name	first_name	last_name
James	Alexander	Jane	Horton
David	Thompson	Jane	Horton
Frances	Drake	Jane	Horton
Alexandria	Link	Mitch	Simmons
Peter	Link	Mitch	Simmons
Antoin	Drake	Paul	Franklin
David	Cruze	NULL	NULL

(7 row(s) affected)

Notice that the only difference between our INNER JOIN and OUTER JOIN statements is the inclusion of David Cruze. As mentioned previously, David Cruze is not assigned to any department supervisor and thus his name shows a NULL value in the list where the columns are identified by each supervisor's first and last name.

In some cases, you may wish to have a table join with itself, say if you want to compare records from within the same table. This is called a self-join. These types of tables are generally found when creating an output list of organizational hierarchies. For example, you may want to find out how many authors live in the same city, so as to provide a list to a publishing house. You could get this output using the following self-join statement:

```
USE pubs
SELECT author1.first_name, author1.last_name, author2.first_name,
       author2.last_name
FROM author1 INNER JOIN author2
ON author1.zip = author2.zip
WHERE author1.city = 'Pittsburgh'
ORDER BY author1.first_name ASC, author1.last_name ASC
```

The resulting output would be as follows:

first_name	last_name	first_name	last_name
David	Jones	David	Jones
David	Jones	Alex	Starr
David	Jones	Linda	Arrow
Alex	Starr	David	Jones
Alex	Starr	Alex	Starr
Alex	Starr	Linda	Arrow
Linda	Arrow	David	Jones
Linda	Arrow	Alex	Starr
Linda	Arrow	Linda	Arrow
Delinda	Burris	Delinda	Burris
Jules	Allan	Jules	Allan

(11 row(s) affected)

If you want to eliminate those rows in which the same author is repeatedly matched, you could make the following change to the self-join query statement:

```
USE pubs
SELECT author1.first_name, author1.last_name, author2.first_name,
       author2.last_name
FROM author1 INNER JOIN author2
ON author1.zip = author2.zip
WHERE author1.city = 'Pittsburgh'
      AND author1.state = 'PA'
      AND author1.author_id < author2.author_id
ORDER BY author1.first_name ASC, author1.last_name ASC
```

The resulting output would be:

first_name	last_name	first_name	last_name
David	Jones	Alex	Starr
David	Jones	Linda	Arrow
Alex	Starr	Linda	Arrow

(3 row(s) affected)

From the results obtained from the query statement, you can confirm that David Jones, Alex Starr, and Linda Arrow all live in Pittsburgh, PA, and have the same ZIP code.

■ Using Queries to Insert Data

THE BOTTOM LINE

In this section, you'll develop an understanding of how data is inserted into a database and how you can use INSERT statements.

Microsoft SQL Server gives you a number of different ways to insert new data into your databases. Different insertion tools are available to achieve the end goal of joining data together.

If you want to insert small quantities of data by adding a few new rows into your database, for instance, you can accomplish this in two different ways. The first method uses the graphical interface too (SSMS), and the second uses the INSERT statement. Either way accomplishes the same goal.

Inserting Data

Let's first learn how to insert data into a table using SSMS before we move on to the syntax method.

INSERT DATA USING SQL SERVER MANAGEMENT STUDIO

GET READY. Before you begin, be sure to launch the SSMS application and connect to the database you wish to work with. Then, follow these steps:

1. Check that you have connected to the database you want to work with (see Figure 3-1).

Figure 3-1

Connecting to the desired database

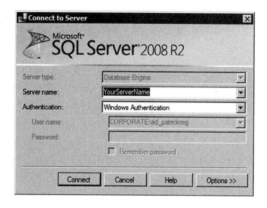

2. Expand the Databases folder by clicking the plus (+) icon beside the word "Databases."
3. Expand the folder of the database you want to modify.
4. Expand the Tables folder by clicking on the plus sign next to the word "Tables."
5. Right-click the table name and chose Edit Top 200 Rows (see Figure 3-2).

Figure 3-2

Edit top 200 rows

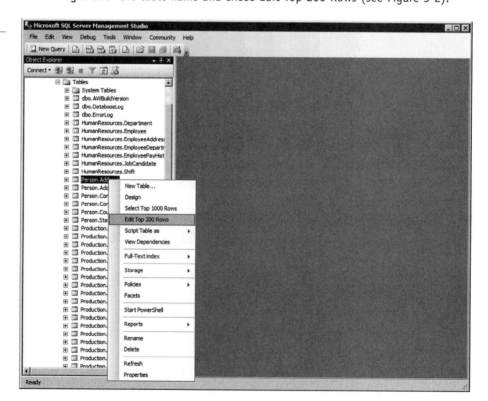

Figure 3-3 shows the output screen. If you have a default value like the IntIdentity field, you will not need to provide the field in your query statement.

Figure 3-3

Edit top 200 rows output screen

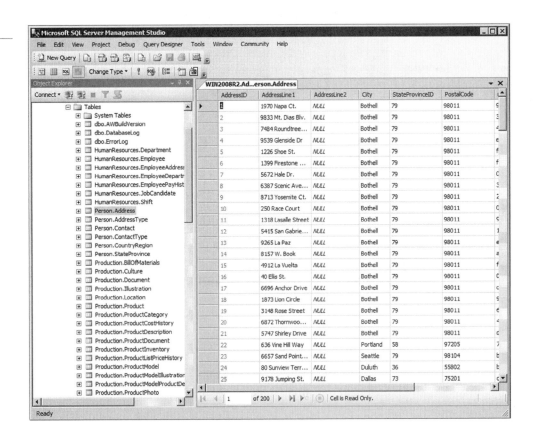

6. Enter your data into the last row of the table for that data to be considered new (or *inserted*) data. The last row of the table will have the value NULL in each of the columns.

PAUSE. Leave the SSMS interface open for the next exercise.

The other method of using the INSERT clause is by writing a SQL statement in the text editor window. With the following syntax, this will provide the same result as using the graphical interface:

INSERT INTO <table_name> (<columns>)

VALUES (<values>)

The <columns> clause would contain your comma-separated list of the column names in the table you wish to include, and the <values> clause would contain the values you would like to insert.

You are not limited to inserting only one row at a time with the INSERT statement; instead, you can indicate multiple rows using a comma to separate them. This is similar to the commas in Excel.CSV files that separate columns of information imported for use in another database program, such as Access. But within an actual INSERT statement, each of the rows identified by commas will be enclosed within parentheses. Thus, an INSERT statement that adds two new employees to our employee table would appear as follows:

INSERT INTO employee (first_name, last_name, employee_id, department)
VALUES ('David', 'Clark', 610008, 'shipping'),
        ('Arnold', 'Davis', 610009, 'accounting')

TAKE NOTE*

Although the columns list in the INSERT statement is entirely optional, it is recommended that you specify what columns you wish to use, as SQL will automatically assume your list of values includes all columns in the correct order.

This will output the following result:

```
(2 row(s) affected)
```

It really is as simple as that to harness the power of database modification and administration. Now, let's explore some other types of data modification.

■ Updating Data and Databases

 THE BOTTOM LINE

As a database administrator, you must understand how data is updated in a database, how to write update data to a database using appropriate UPDATE statements, and how to update a database using a table.

CERTIFICATION READY
What command is used to change existing data in a table?
3.3

The function of the UPDATE statement is to change data in a table or view. Much like any of the data manipulation or modification clauses and statements within SQL, you can use this statement in either SSMS or a text editor window.

Using the UPDATE Statement

The UPDATE clause allows you to modify data stored in tables using data attributes such as the following:

```
UPDATE <table_name>
SET <attribute> = <value>
WHERE <conditions>
```

As you've seen from the beginning of this lesson, you can read this type of SQL statement much as you would any sentence. Say you want to update a table in which you want a certain column identifier to reflect a certain value. Perhaps you want to have an attribute of a new supervisor (think of our employee example), Doug Able, being assigned to new employees for training purposes. That supervisor could have the attribute set for him or her as (looking back at our department table) an ID of 4, and the WHERE clause would be satisfied by having it match the NULL condition for our employees without a supervisor. Let's write that scenario UPDATE statement to update the previous example.

The first step would be to add a record in the department table with our new supervisor's name and department ID information using the INSERT statement:

```
INSERT INTO department (first_name, last_name, department_id)
VALUES ('Doug', 'Able', 4)
```

The output response would be as follows:

```
(1 row(s) affected)
```

TAKE NOTE*
If you don't specify what records to update, all records or rows will be updated with the new value. This is potentially harmful.

Now, we need to update our employee table to reflect any employees who do not have an assigned department supervisor. Here, our UPDATE statement would look as follows:

```
UPDATE employee
SET department = 4
WHERE department IS NULL
```

The result is shown in Table 3-4.

Table 3-4

NULL values in the department column

92	2010-04-03....	Dbo	CREATE_VIEW	dbo	vDVMPrep	CREATE VIEW [...	<EVENT_INSTA...
92	2010-04-03....	Dbo	CREATE_VIEW	dbo	vTimeSeries	CREATE VIEW [...	<EVENT_INSTA...
92	2010-04-03....	dbo	CREATE_VIEW	dbo	vTargetMail	CREATE VIEW [...	<EVENT_INSTA...
NULL	*NULL*	*NULL*	*NULL*	*NULL*	*NULL*	*NULL*	*NULL*

Referring back to Table 3-1, notice that only one employee, David Cruze, did not have a department ID number assigned to him, meaning his value was NULL in the department column. Because we added a new supervisor to the department table in our INSERT INTO statement above, David Cruze now has an identified department number and has Doug Able as his assigned supervisor.

In comparison, to update a table using the SSMS graphical interface, you simply need to follow these steps:

- Open the SSMS interface.
- Open the table in which you wish to update data.
- Locate the row in which you wish to update the records within the Open Table view.

■ Deleting Data

THE BOTTOM LINE

All database administrators must understand how to delete data from single or multiple tables, as well how to ensure data and referential integrity by using transactions.

CERTIFICATION READY
What commands are used to delete data from a database?
3.4

There are several different ways to remove rows from a table or view. You can identify and delete individual rows from the database using the DELETE syntax, delete all the rows using a `truncate table` statement, or remove the entire table using the `drop table` statement. Which method you choose depends entirely on your needs or the amount of data you need to remove.

Using the DELETE Statement

TAKE NOTE*

Rows are not actually deleted from the table source (table_source) identified in the FROM clause, only from the table named in the DELETE clause (table_ or_view).

You can use the DELETE statement to remove one or more rows in a table or view. This statement is structured as follows:

```
DELETE FROM <table_name>
WHERE <conditions>
```

You can use the DELETE statement in a variety of situations. For instance, you could delete all accounting department employees from a company's employee table if, because of a corporate takeover, they are no longer no longer employed by the company. You could delete this information using the following command:

```
DELETE FROM employee
WHERE department = 'accounting'
```

This would return the following value:

```
(1 row(s) affected)
```

This result shows that the one employee who worked in the accounting department has now been removed from the employee table.

Truncating a Table with TRUNCATE TABLE

Perhaps you would like to delete all the rows from a particular table. You could use the TRUNCATE TABLE statement to do this, although you may also be tempted to use DELETE and the where condition. This latter technique would produce the same output, but it could take a great deal of time if you are deleting rows from very large databases. Thus, the TRUNCATE TABLE statement would be the better option. The syntax of the statement looks like this:

```
TRUNCATE TABLE <table_name>
```

Each successfully executed result from SQL will appear as follows:

```
Command(s) completed successfully.
```

The TRUNCATE TABLE statement removes the actual data from within the table, but it leaves the table structure in place for future use.

Deleting a Table with DROP TABLE

Perhaps you want to delete an entire table because it is obsolete, because it contains too much data to move around, or for some other reason. Removing an entire table involves use of the DROP TABLE statement, which looks like this:

```
DROP TABLE <table_name>
```

Using Referential Integrity

One of the most important steps in planning a database, creating tables, manipulating data, and so forth is setting up a proper security model, of which referential integrity forms a part. A larger problem in database manipulation and maintenance is that sometimes SQL Server data is lost and must be recovered. If proper safeguards are not in place as part of the backup and recovery process, recovering lost data could prove a very harrowing ordeal.

One safeguard measure that can be taken with regard to database tables is the use of referential integrity practice methods. One of the most common mistakes in database manipulation is the accidental loss of entire tables. The best way to avoid this type of situation in the first place is to ensure that your database uses *referential integrity*. Referential integrity does not allow deletion of tables unless all of the related tables are deleted using a cascading delete.

This brings us to another best-practice method: using *transactions* when updating data. Data is most commonly deleted, truncated, or accidentally updated during regular maintenance tasks, and one of the best ways to keep this from occurring is to use transactions when updating data. Inserting a simple begin tran before an actual SQL statement is a good place to start, and if you have executed everything correctly, a COMMIT statement is issued from SQL. If there is an error in any of the statements, a ROLLBACK is issued from SQL.

A sample transaction statement might appear as follows:

```
BEGIN TRAN
DELETE FROM <table_name>
```

What happens at this juncture is that you would verify that what you did really did happen and then issue a COMMIT statement to save those changes, or else issue a ROLLBACK to undo them. Many times mistakes occur through simple errors, and if you use the BEGIN TRAN and a COMMIT or ROLLBACK while performing maintenance tasks, you will catch most accidents before they happen.

SKILL SUMMARY

IN THIS LESSON, YOU LEARNED THE FOLLOWING:

- The SQL command for retrieving any data from a database is SELECT.
- There are only three things you need to identify in your statement in order to form a proper SELECT query: what columns to retrieve, what tables to retrieve them from, and what conditions, if any, the data must satisfy.
- A BETWEEN clause allows you to specify the range to be used in a "between x and y" query format.
- The NOT keyword is used to search data in terms of what you don't want in your output.
- The UNION clause allows you to combine the results of any two or more queries into a resulting single set that will include all the rows belonging to the query in that union.
- The EXCEPT clause returns any distinct values from the left query that are not also found on the right query, whereas the INTERSECT clause returns any distinct values not found on both the left and right sides of this operand.
- The JOIN clause allows you to combine related data from multiple table sources.
- To insert data, you can use SSMS or the INSERT statement.
- The function of the UPDATE statement is to change data in a table or a view.
- The DELETE statement removes rows from a table or a view.
- The TRUNCATE TABLE statement removes data from within a table but leaves the table structure in place for future use.
- An entire table can be removed with the DROP TABLE command. The best way to avoid the accidental deletion of entire tables is to use referential integrity. Referential integrity does not allow deletion of tables unless all of the related tables are deleted using a cascading delete.

Knowledge Assessment

True or False

Circle T if the statement is true or F if the statement is false

T | F　**1.** The SELECT statement is limited to querying data from a single table.

T | F　**2.** The INSERT statement can be used to insert multiple rows at a time.

T | F　**3.** The TRUNCATE statement is used to delete a table.

T | F　**4.** An INNER JOIN condition is the same as a CROSS JOIN and a WHERE condition.

T | F　**5.** The order of the columns in a SELECT statement must match the order in which the columns were created when the table was made.

Fill in the Blank

Complete the following sentences by writing the correct word or words in the blanks provided.

1. The SELECT statement is used to query and combine data from one or more _____.

2. The WHERE clause of a SELECT statement contains one or more _____ for filtering the data being queried.

3. Using the _____ statement is the most efficient way to delete all rows from a table.

4. To combine the results of two queries, use the _____ operator.

5. Use the _____ statement to modify one or more rows in a table.

6. By using the _____ and a _____ or _____ while performing maintenance tasks, you will catch most accidents before they happen.

7. The removal of an entire table can be accomplished using the _____ and _____ syntax.

8. To select a single column for your query, identify the name of the column by typing it between the _____ and _____ words in the query statement.

9. You can _____ several conditions in one query statement to satisfy your requirements.

10. The _____ clause allows you to combine the results of any two or more queries into a resulting single set that will include all the rows belonging to the query.

Multiple Choice

Circle the letter that corresponds to the best answer.

1. Which of the following conditions is invalid?
   a. salary <> 50000
   b. salary != 50000
   c. salary NOT EQUAL 50000
   d. NOT salary = 50000

2. Which of the following operators is not supported when combining results between SELECT statements?
   a. UNION
   b. EXCEPT
   c. INTERSECT
   d. AND

3. Which of the following range conditions would generate a syntax error?
   a. salary <= 50000 and salary >= 10000
   b. salary between (10000 and 50000) and (60000 and 90000)
   c. salary >= 10000 and salary <= 50000
   d. salary between 10000 and 50000

4. Which of the following will combine the results of two or more queries into a resulting single set that includes all the rows belonging to the query?
   a. UNION
   b. EXCEPT
   c. INTERSECT
   d. AND

5. Which of the following is used to prevent accidental deletion of data in a table?
   a. Transactions
   b. Null values
   c. Inner joins
   d. Referential integrity

■ Competency Assessment

Scenario 3-1: Using the SELECT Command

You have just have been hired as a database administrator for the AdventureWorks Corporation. A network administrator wants to know how to extract information from the AdventureWorks database. Therefore, you need to answer the following questions:

1. What command would you use to display records from a table?

2. What command would you use to display a FirstName and LastName from the Users table?

3. What command would you use to display all records from the Member database and have it sorted by the Name column?

4. What command would you use to display all records from the Suppliers table that have the City of Sacramento?

5. What command would you use to display the CompanyName, ContactName, and PhoneNumber from the Suppliers table with Supplier ID greater than 1000?

6. What command would you use to display CompanyName, ContactName, and Phone Number from the Customers table for companies that have more than 100 employees and reside in the state of California?

Scenario 3-2: Deleting Data from Tables

After you and the network administrator review some records in the AdventureWorks database, the two of you decide to delete some old records. This scenario brings up the following questions:

1. What command would you use to remove all records from the Customer table where the age is less than 18?

2. What command would you use to remove all records from the Schools table that have enrollment less than 500?

3. What command would you use to remove all records from the Contact table that do not have a country of USA and at the same time free the space used by those records?

4. What command would you use to delete the Temp table?

■ Proficiency Assessment

Scenario 3-3: Manipulating Data Using SELECT and JOIN Statements

You are a database administrator for the AdventureWorks Corporation. Some confusion has arisen because the company's purchase orders are stored in two tables. Therefore, you need to write a query to join the PurchaseOrderHeader table in the sample database, AdventureWorks, to itself in order to provide a list of purchase orders paired together. Each row includes two purchase orders that have identical vendors and shipping methods.

1. After opening SSMS and accessing the AdventureWorks database, what query would you use against the AdventureWorks database to display the ProductSubcategoryID and ProductCategoryID from the Production.ProductSub table that contain the word "Bike"? You also want to sort by Subcategory Name.

2. What query would you use to join the ProductCategory table to the ProductSubcategory table in order to retrieve the Name column from within the ProductCategory table?

Scenario 3-4: Manipulating Data Using INSERT and UPDATE Statements

As the AdventureWorks DBA, you need to insert data into the Credit table in the Sales database using a variety of data statements, along with updating and deleting data from the same Credit table.

1. After opening SSMS, what commands would you type and execute in the AdventureWorks database to review the columns in the Sales table?

2. In the existing query window, what commands would you use that will add the following row to the Credit table?

   Patrick, Roberts, 6000, Roberts@telecome.usa

3. In the existing query window, what commands would you type, highlight, and execute to add the following rows to the Credit table for firstname, lastname, and credit limit?

   Alex, Hall, 5000

   Annie, Smith, 10000

4. In the existing query window, what commands would you use to update the email address (Email) for Annie Smith in the Credit table using the Update statement?

Understanding Data Storage

OBJECTIVE DOMAIN MATRIX

SKILLS/CONCEPTS	MTA EXAM OBJECTIVE	MTA EXAM OBJECTIVE NUMBER
Normalizing a Database	Understand normalization.	4.1
Understanding Primary, Foreign and Composite Keys	Understand primary, foreign, and composite keys.	4.2
Understanding Clustered and Non-Clustered Indexes	Understand indexes.	4.3

KEY TERMS

clustered index

composite primary key

fifth normal form (5NF)

first normal form (1NF)

foreign key

foreign key constraint

form

fourth normal form (4NF)

non-clustered index

normalization

normal forms (NF)

primary key

redundant data

second normal form (2NF)

third normal form (3NF)

unique key constraint

You work for a large warehouse distribution company that provides outdoor camping equipment to over 90 stores in North America. You have just received an office memo stating that the company has purchased a second store in the state of Washington. Your boss has asked you to add a new table to the database for this store, saying that the table should be populated with the same equipment that is sold in the first Washington store. She wants to ensure both that database integrity is maintained and that the new table remains normalized to the third normal form.

In this lesson, you will learn about database normalization, the five most common levels of normalization, and the purpose of normalization as it relates to database integrity. You will also learn why foreign, primary, and composite keys play an integral role in referential integrity.

■ Normalizing a Database

 THE BOTTOM LINE
As a database administrator, you must understand the reasons for normalization, the five most common levels of normalization, and how to normalize a database to the third normal form.

TAKE NOTE ∗

Normalization is the elimination of redundant data to save space.

CERTIFICATION READY
What are the first three normalization forms, and how do they differ from one another?
4.1

The main reason for using normalization techniques in data storage arose in the days when storage cost a great deal more than it does today. Indeed, *normalization*, in a nutshell, is the elimination of *redundant data* to save space.

Now that you understand the general definition of normalization, let's look more closely at this concept and its application in database design.

Understanding Normalization

Normalization is based entirely on the data design and organization processes that are derived from the rules used when building and designing relational databases. Therefore, understanding what relational databases are and the importance of good design methodologies is extremely important.

Normalization, by definition, is the process of organizing data in order to reduce redundancy by dividing a database into two or more tables and then defining table relationships. The objective of this operation is to isolate data so that additions, deletions, and modifications occurring in each field can be made inside one table and then propagated throughout the rest of the database using these defined relationships.

There are five *normalization forms (NFs)*, of which we'll focus on the first three:

- **First normalization form (1NF):** Eliminate repeating groups
- **Second normalization form (2NF):** Eliminate redundant data
- **Third normalization form (3NF):** Eliminate columns not dependent on key
- **Fourth normalization form (4NF):** Isolate independent multiple relationships
- **Fifth normalization form (5NF):** Isolate semantically related multiple relationships

Let's now look at each one of these forms in a little more depth. Taking a detailed look at the normal forms moves this lesson into a more formal study of relational database design. Contrary to popular opinion, the forms are not a progressive methodology, but they do represent a progressive level of compliance. Technically, you can't be in 2NF until you have met 1NF; therefore, don't plan on designing an entity and moving it through the first normal form to the second normal form, and so on, because each normal form is simply a different type of data integrity with different requirements that must be fulfilled.

Understanding the First Normal Form

The *first normalized form (1NF)* means the data is in an entity format, which basically means that the following three conditions must be met:

- The table must have no duplicate records. Once you have defined a primary key for the table, you have met the first normalized form criterion.
- The table also must not have multivalued attributes, meaning that you can't combine in a single column multiple values that are considered valid for a column. For an example

of the first normal form in action, consider the listing of base camps and tours from the Cape Hatteras Adventures database. Table 4-1 shows the base camp data in a model that violates the first normal form: the repeating tour attribute (Tour 1, Tour 2, and Tour 3) is not unique. In other words, there are three values assigned for Tours.

- The entries in the column or attribute must be of the same data type.

Table 4-1

Base camp data (before): Violating the first normal form

BASECAMP	TOUR1	TOUR2	TOUR3
Asheville	Appalachian Trail	Blue Ridge Parkway Hike	
Cape Hatteras	Outer Banks Lighthouses		
Freeport	Bahamas Dive		
Ft. Lauderdale	Amazon Trek		
West Virginia	Gauley River Rafting		

To redesign the data model so that it complies with the first normal form, you must resolve the repeating group of tour attributes into a single unique attribute, as shown in Table 4-2, and then move any multiple values to a unique table. Here, the BaseCamp entity contains a unique table for each base camp, and the Tour entity's BaseCampID refers to the primary key in the BaseCamp entity.

Table 4-2

Base camp data (after): Conforming to the first normal form

TOUR ENTITY		BASECAMP ENTITY	
BASECAMPID (FK)	TOUR	BASECAMPID (PK)	NAME
1	Appalachian Trail	1	Asheville
1	Blue Ridge Parkway Hike	2	Cape Hatteras
2	Outer Banks Lighthouses	3	Freeport
3	Bahamas Dive	4	Ft. Lauderdale
4	Amazon Trek	5	
5	Gauley River Rafting		

Understanding the Second Normal Form

The *second normal form (2NF)* ensures that each attribute does in fact describe the entity. This form is entirely based on dependency: specifically, the attributes of the entity in question, which is not part of a candidate key, must be functionally dependent upon the entire primary key. What ends up happening on occasion is that combined primary keys run into trouble with the second normal form if the attributes aren't dependent on every attribute in the primary key. If an attribute depends on one of the primary key attributes but not the others, then it becomes a partial dependency, which violates the second normal form.

To better understand violations of the second normal form, Table 4-3 shows an example of the same base camp data when it is not in 2NF, and Table 4-4 shows the same data after it has been conformed.

Table 4-3

Base camp data (before): Violating the second normal form

PK-BaseCamp	PK-Tour	Base Camp PhoneNumber
Asheville	Appalachian Trail	828-555-1212
Asheville	Blue Ridge Parkway Hike	828-555-1212
Cape Hatteras	Outer Banks Lighthouses	828-555-1213
Freeport	Bahamas Dive	828-555-1214
Ft. Lauderdale	Amazon Trek	828-555-1215
West Virginia	Gauley River Rafting	828-555-1216

Table 4-4

Base camp data (after): Conforming to the second normal form

Tour Entity		Base Camp Entity	
PK-Base Camp	PK-Tour	BK-Base Camp	PhoneNumber
Asheville	Appalachian Trail	Asheville	828-555-1212
Asheville	Blue Ridge Parkway Hike	Cape Hatteras	828-555-1213
Cape Hatteras	Outer Banks Lighthouses	Freeport	828-555-1214
Freeport	Bahamas Dive	Ft. Lauderdale	828-555-1215
Ft. Lauderdale	Amazon Trek	West Virginia	828-555-1216
West Virginia	Gauley River Rafting		

Understanding the Third Normal Form

The *third normal form (3NF)* checks for transitive dependencies. A transitive dependency is similar to a partial dependency in that both refer to attributes that are not fully dependent on a primary key. A dependency is considered transient when attribute1 is dependent on attribute2, which is then dependent on the primary key.

When looking at whether there is a violation in either the second or third normal form, remember that each attribute is directly or indirectly tied to the primary key. Therefore, the second normal form is violated when an attribute depends on only part of the key, and the third normal form is violated when the attribute depends on the key but also on another nonkey attribute. The central phrase to remember in describing the third normal form is that every attribute must "provide a fact about the key, the whole key, and nothing but the key." Just as with the second normal form, the third normal form is resolved by moving the nondependent attribute to a new entity.

To better understand violations of the third normal form, Table 4-5 shows an example of the same base camp data when it is not in 3NF, and Table 4-6 shows the data after it has been conformed.

Table 4-5

Base camp data (before): Violating the third normal form

BASE CAMP ENTITY			
BASECAMPPK	**BASECAMPPHONENUMBER**	**LEADGUIDE**	**DATEOFHIRE**
Asheville	1-828-555-1212	Jeff Davis	5/1/99
Cape Hatteras	1-828-555-1213	Ken Frank	4/15/97
Freeport	1-828-555-1215	Dab Smith	7/7/2001
Ft. Lauderdale	1-828-555-1215	Sam Wilson	1/1/2002
West Virginia	1-828-555-1216	Lauren Jones	6/1/2000

Table 4-6

Base camp data (after): Conforming to the third normal form

TOUR ENTITY		LEADGUIDE ENTITY	
BASECAMPPK	**LEADGUIDE**	**LEADGUIDEPK**	**DATEOFHIRE**
Asheville	Jeff Davis	Jeff Davis	5/1/99
Cape Hatteras	Ken Frank	Ken Frank	4/15/97
Freeport	Dab Smith	Dab Smith	7/7/2001
West Virginia	Lauren Jones	Lauren Jones	6/1/2000

HOW TO NORMALIZE A DATABASE TO THE THIRD NORMAL FORM

There are two basic requirements for a database to be in third normal form:

- The database must already meet the requirements of both 1NF and 2NF.
- The database must not contain any columns that aren't fully dependent upon the primary key.

In order to understand how a database can be put into the third normal form, let's imagine that we have a table of widget orders that contains the following attributes:

- Order Number (primary key)
- Customer Number
- Unit Price
- Quantity
- Total

Remember, our first requirement is that the table must satisfy the requirements of both 1NF and 2NF. Are there any duplicative columns? No. Do we have a primary key? Yes, the order number. Therefore, we satisfy the requirements of 1NF. Are there any subsets of data that apply to multiple rows? No, so we also satisfy the requirements of 2NF.

Now, are all the columns fully dependent upon the primary key? The customer number varies with the order number, and it doesn't appear to depend on any of the other fields. What about the unit price? This field could be dependent on the customer number in a situation where we charged each customer a set price. However, from the information provided in the table fields, we can sometimes charge the same customer different prices. Therefore, the unit price is fully dependent on the order number. The quantity of items also varies from order to order, so we're okay there.

What about the total? It looks as if we might be in trouble here. The total can be derived by multiplying the unit price by the quantity, and therefore it's not fully dependent on the primary key. We must remove it from the table to comply with the third normal form. Perhaps we could replace our original attributes with the following attributes:

- Order Number
- Customer Number
- Unit Price
- Quantity

Now our table is in 3NF. But, you might ask, what about the total? This is a derived field, and it's best not to store it in the database at all. We can simply compute it "on the fly" when performing database queries. For example, we might have previously used this query to retrieve order numbers and totals:

```
SELECT OrderNumber, Total
FROM WidgetOrders
```

We can now use the following query in order to achieve the same results, without violating normalization rules:

```
SELECT OrderNumber, UnitPrice * Quantity AS Total
FROM WidgetOrders
```

Understanding the Fourth Normal Form

The *fourth normal form (4NF)* involves two independent attributes brought together to form a primary key along with a third attribute. But, if the two attributes don't really uniquely identify the entity without the third attribute, then the design violates the fourth normal form.

Understanding the Fifth Normal Form

The *fifth normal form (5NF)* provides a method for designing complex relationships involving multiple (usually three or more) entities.

Typically, database administrators feel that satisfying the requirements of the first, second, and third normal forms is enough. The fourth and fifth normal forms may be complex, but violating them can cause severe problems.

It is important to look at database design as a whole and not just as designing something to fulfill half of the needs of your users, employers, and so forth. It's not necessarily whether a number of entities are used or not used; rather, it's a matter of properly aligning the attributes and keys. Any violation of the normal forms can cause a cascading effect with multiple violations and inefficient databases.

Normalization reduces locking contention and improves multiple-user performance. Locks are essential mechanisms that are used to prevent simultaneous changes to the database, such as two different users making changes to the same record. Without locks, a change made by one transaction could be overwritten by another transaction that executes at the same time. Last, normalization has these three advantages:

- **Development costs:** Although it may take longer to design a normalized database, such databases are easier to work with and reduce development costs.
- **Usability:** Placing columns in the correct table makes it easier to understand a database and write correct queries. This helps reduce design time and cost.
- **Extensibility:** A non-normalized database is often more complex and therefore more difficult to modify. This leads to delays in rolling out new databases and increases in development costs.

■ Understanding Primary, Foreign, and Composite Keys

THE BOTTOM LINE

In this section, you'll learn about the reasons for using keys in a database. You'll also explore how to choose appropriate primary keys, select appropriate data types for keys, select appropriate fields for composite keys, and understand the relationship between foreign and primary keys.

CERTIFICATION READY
What are the differences between a primary key and a foreign key?
4.2

Three different types of constraints available within SQL Server ensure that you are able to maintain database integrity: primary keys, foreign keys, and composite (unique) keys. A *unique key constraint* will allow you to enforce the uniqueness property of columns, in addition to a primary key within a table. A unique constraint acts similarly to a primary key but with two important differences:

- Columns containing a unique key constraint may contain only one row with a NULL value. You cannot have two rows containing a NULL value in the same option, as that would violate the unique constraint's duplicate value error.
- A table may have multiple unique constraints.

 CREATE A UNIQUE CONSTRAINT

GET READY. Before you begin this exercise, be sure to launch the SQL Server Management Studio application and connect to the database you wish to work with. Then, follow these steps:

1. Using SQL Server Management Studio, open the table in which you want to create the constraint in Design View. You can do so by right-clicking the table and selecting Design from the menu that appears, as shown in Figure 4-1.

Figure 4-1

Design view

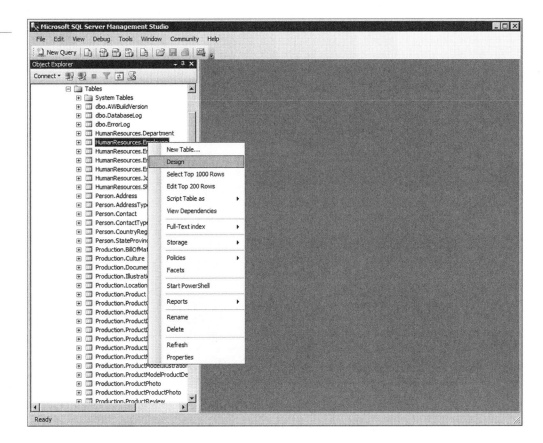

2. From the Table Designer drop-down menu at the top of the toolbar, select Indexes/Keys, as shown in Figure 4-2. This opens the Indexes/Keys window. You will notice that the table already has a primary key constraint identified, as shown in Figure 4-3.

Figure 4-2

Indexes/Keys

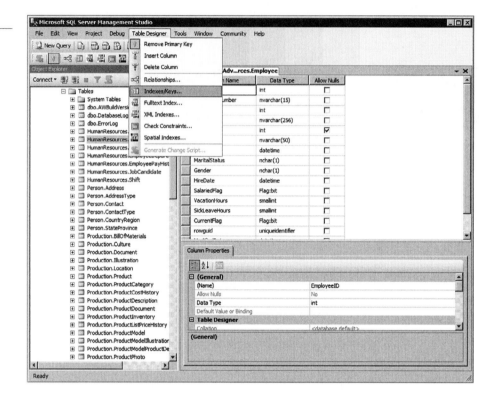

Figure 4-3

Connecting to a database

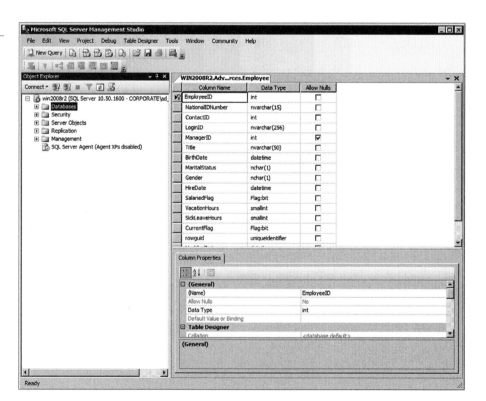

3. Click on the Add button to create a new key.

4. Click the Type property in the right side of the property box and change it from the default of Index to Unique Key, as shown in Figure 4-4.

Figure 4-4

Type property box

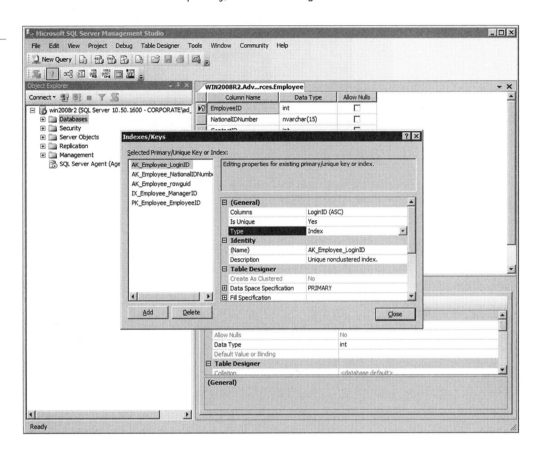

5. Click the ellipsis (. . .), which is found beside the Columns property section. See Figure 4-5. You can now select the columns you wish to include in your unique constraint.

Figure 4-5

Selecting columns to add

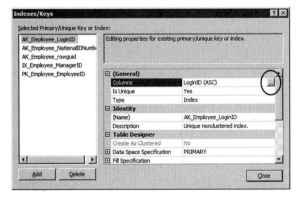

6. Click the Close button.

7. Save your newly created constraint by selecting Save all from the File menu, as shown in Figure 4-6.

Figure 4-6

Saving a new constraint

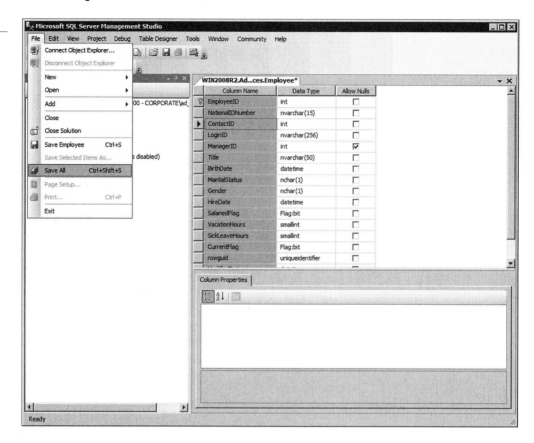

You have now created your own unique constraint.

PAUSE. Leave the SSMS interface open for the next exercise.

Understanding Primary Keys

Perhaps the most important concept of designing any database table is ensuring that it has a *primary key*—in other words, an attribute or set of attributes that can be used to uniquely identify each row. Every table must have a primary key; without a primary key, it's not a valid table. By definition, a primary key must be unique and must have a value that is not null.

In some tables, there might be multiple possible primary keys to choose from, such as employee number, driver's license number, or another government-issued number such as a Social Security number (SSN). In this case, all the potential primary keys are known as candidate keys. Candidate keys that are not selected as the primary key are then known as alternate keys.

Remember, in the initial database diagramming phase, a primary key might be readily visible—for instance, it could be an employee number or a manufacturer name; however, more often than not, there is no clearly recognizable, uniquely identifying value for each item in most real-world scenarios.

Understanding Foreign Keys

Throughout the lessons in this book, you have been inundated with the terminology of relational databases. This terminology also carries forward into the use of index keys, such as *foreign keys*. When two tables relate to each other, one of them will act as the primary table and the other will act as the secondary table. In order to connect the two tables, the primary key is replicated from the primary to the secondary table, and all the key attributes duplicated from the primary table become known as the foreign key. Although this may at times be referred to as a parent-child relationship, enforcing the foreign key attribute is actually referred to as referential integrity (refer to the discussion in the previous lesson of referential integrity).

To get a better visual idea of this type of relationship, look at Figure 4-7, which shows an order's primary key duplicated in the order detail table, thus providing the link between the two tables.

Figure 4-7

Primary key duplication

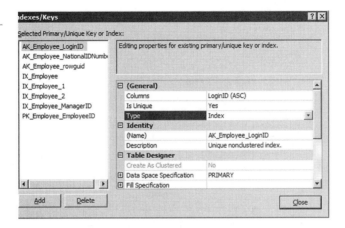

When discussing foreign keys and primary keys, the terminology will almost always include the constraint as part of the description. As an example of the role of the *foreign key constraint*, let's consider a retail store database. Each store has a table containing information about that store, such as employee information, products sold, inventory on hand, and more than likely information about customers. One way to reference the table data logically would be to create a Unit_Number field within the Employees table that would then contain the Unit_Number (the primary key of the Stores table) of the employee's store, thus creating a link between the two tables.

Is this a logical setup or not? Ask yourself what would happen if one of the stores closed in the future. In this situation, it's likely that all the employees associated with the store would be "orphaned," as they would be associated with a Unit_Number field that no longer exists. There is also the potential for human error—for instance, someone may inadvertently type an incorrect Unit_Number while entering an employee into the database, thus creating a number for a store that doesn't exist. This could prove a problem for payroll or other human resources actions.

These types of problems are referred to as relational integrity issues, as you learned in the previous lesson. Thankfully, SQL Server provides the necessary foreign key constraint to prevent this type of error. A foreign key then creates a relationship between two tables by linking the foreign key in one of the tables to the primary key of the referenced table.

TAKE NOTE*

Every table must have a primary key; without a primary key, it's not a valid table. By definition, a primary key must be unique and must have a value that is not null.

CREATE A FOREIGN KEY USING SQL SERVER MANAGEMENT STUDIO

GET READY. To create a foreign key constraint using the SSMS interface, follow these steps. Before you begin, be sure to launch the SQL Server Management Studio application and connect to the database you want to work with.

1. In SSMS, open the table in which you wish to create a foreign key. Right-click the table and select Design view, as shown in Figure 4-8.

Figure 4-8

Design view

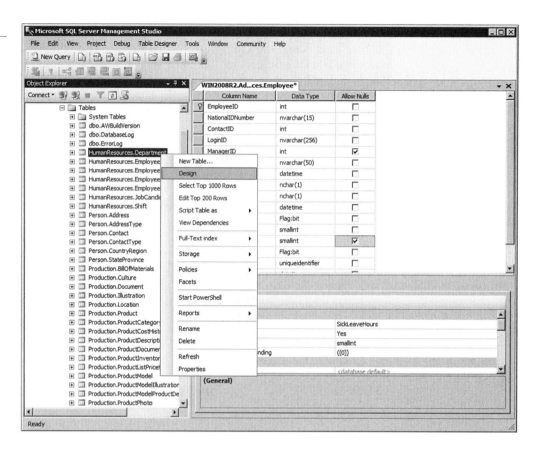

2. Select Relationships from the Table Designer drop-down menu, as shown in Figure 4-9.

Figure 4-9

Selecting Relationships

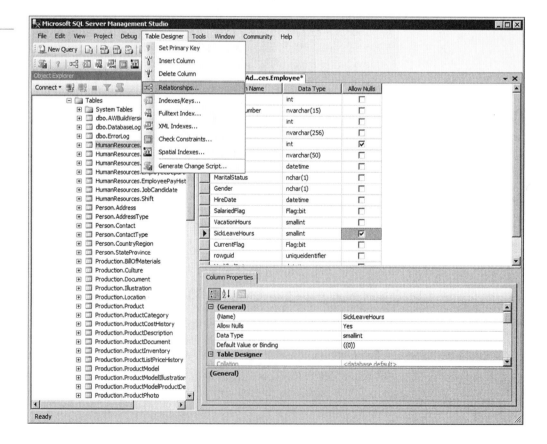

3. Select the table to which you wish to add the foreign key constraint.

4. Click the ellipsis (. . .) beside the Tables and Columns Specification property dialog box, as shown in Figure 4-10.

Figure 4-10

Tables and Columns
Specification Box

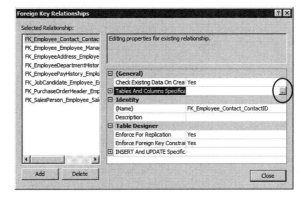

5. Select the table that your foreign key refers to in the primary key table drop-down list, as shown in Figure 4-11.

Figure 4-11

Selecting the table your foreign
key refers to

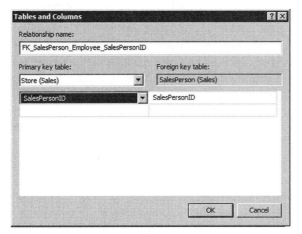

6. Once you have completed adding the foreign key table information, click OK to close the dialog box.

7. Click the Close button.

8. Save your newly created constraint by selecting Save all from the File menu.

PAUSE. Leave the SSMS interface open for the next exercise.

Now that this foreign key relationship has been created between two tables, SQL Server will require all associated values with the constraint in the foreign key table to have corresponding values in the primary key table. This does not require that the opposite happen (i.e., that the primary key have corresponding values in the foreign key table.) Remember, multiple values in the foreign key table can reference the same record in the primary key table.

Understanding Composite Primary Keys

One of the most confusing issues regarding primary keys is the definition of a composite primary key. A *composite primary key* occurs when you define more than one column as your primary key. Although many database administrators do not use composite primary keys and are not aware of them, they play an integral part in designing a good, solid data model.

As a simplified example, imagine that you take the tables in a database and categorize them based on two data types:

- Tables that *define* entities
- Tables that *relate* entities

The tables that define entities are the tables defining such things as customers, salespersons, and transactions related to sales. You can choose any column in these tables as a primary key, because in this discussion of composite primary keys, tables that define entities are not an important topic.

It is in the tables that relate entities that the composite primary key plays an important role. Using our previous example, suppose you have a system in place that tracks customers, and this system allows you to assign multiple products to multiple customers in order to indicate what they can or cannot order. You are thus looking at a "many-to-many" relationship between the Customer and Products tables. You already have a table for Customers and one for Products, and you also have a primary key selected for the ProductID column of the Products table and the CustomerID column of the Customers table. Next, you would need to look at how to define your CustomerProducts table.

The CustomerProducts table relates the customers to products, so the purpose of this table is to relate the two entities that have already been defined within the database. Oftentimes, when a database administrator is designing a table for the first time, much thought goes into ensuring that data integrity is at the forefront of the design guidelines; yet by ensuring the table's primary key is identified, a database administrator does ensure that data integrity is maintained. The bottom line is that in order to maintain data integrity, the primary key must form part of the design requirements for each table.

Many times a table is not designed to take into account the possible duplication of data inputs, and although many think that the UI (unique identifier) can handle any data duplication, an update to the table data can always occur, such as when a system is upgraded and data must be moved over, or some transaction must be restored from a backup. Hence, there is a necessity to ensure that data integrity is maintained.

If you begin to look at table design with an understanding of data integrity and defining a table's primary key, you will see that using a unique constraint will ensure that integrity is maintained. Remember, a primary key is a set of columns in a table that uniquely identifies each row of data.

■ Understanding Clustered and Non-Clustered Indexes

THE BOTTOM LINE

In this section, you'll learn about clustered and non-clustered indexes and their purpose in a database.

CERTIFICATION READY
What is the difference between a clustered and a non-clustered index?
4.3

As a database administrator, you should understand what the two types of indexes (clustered and non-clustered) do and what the role of these indexes is within a database environment. You're probably already familiar with the index in a textbook, which contains entries for particular subjects, words, and ideas. Whenever you want to quickly find information in the book, you can simply turn to this index. Indexing with databases, in the larger scheme of things, is exactly the same thing.

In SQL Server, to retrieve data from a database, SQL server checks each row to look for the query on which you were trying to find information. Does this sound like an incredible amount of time spent inefficiently? If you answered yes, you would be correct! Thus, what SQL Server does (with the help of database administrators) is build and maintain a variety of indexes in order to locate and return commonly used fields quickly.

The only real drawbacks to indexing are the time it takes to build the actual indexes and the storage space the indexes require. One important decision in using indexes is figuring out what indexes are appropriate for your database, based on the types of queries you will perform. Remember, SQL Server allows you to create your indexes on either single or multiple columns, but the real speed gain will be on those indexes based on the column(s) inside the index.

Understanding Clustered Indexes

TAKE NOTE *

Only one clustered index is allowed for each table.

When you begin looking at implementing indexes, it is important to remember that each table can have only one *clustered index* that defines how SQL Server will sort the data stored inside the table. After all, because that data can only be sorted in one way, it simply is not possible to have two clustered indexes on the same table. It should also be mentioned that a clustered index is a physical construct, unlike most indexes, which are logical or software-based.

One important feature of SQL Server is its automatic creation of a clustered index when the primary key is defined for a table. A primary key makes it simple for you, as database administrator, to look at creating non-clustered indexes based on the columns in a table.

So far we have given a simplistic overview of what indexes are and why they are created. It is important now to look at the basics of an index. An index is an on-disk (or stored) structure associated entirely with a table or a view that increases the speed of data retrieval. In order to create an index, a series of keys is built from one or more columns in each row within a table or a view. These keys are then stored in a structure called a B-tree that enables SQL Server to find the row(s) associated with those defined values much more quickly and efficiently. Figure 4-12 shows an example of a B-tree structure.

Figure 4-12

B-tree structure

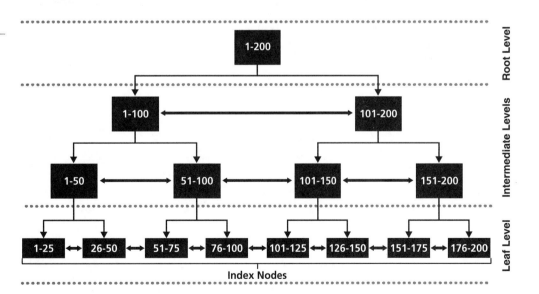

In a clustered index, the data is sorted and stored in the table or view that is based on their respective key values. These columns are included within the index definition, and because the data in the rows themselves are sorted in only one order, this is why, as mentioned above, you can only have one clustered index per table.

A table with a clustered index is considered a clustered table; when a table has no clustered index, the data rows are then stored in an unordered structure called a heap. This brings us to the definition of a non-clustered index.

Understanding Non-Clustered Indexes

You have the freedom to create your own non-clustered indexes because they have a structure different from the clustered index structure. This is because a ***non-clustered index*** contains the non-clustered index key values, and each of those keys has a pointer to a data row that contains the key value. This pointer is referred to as a row locator, and the locator's structure depends on whether the data pages are stored in a heap or as a clustered table. This is an important part of a non-clustered index's function: if it points to a heap, the row locator is a pointer to the row, but in a clustered table, the row locator is then the clustered index key.

Creating a Non-Clustered Index on a Table

There are two ways to create a non-clustered index on a table. One uses Transact-SQL script statements, and the other uses the visual interface of SQL Server Management Studio. As a database administrator, you should know how to create indexes either way.

 CREATE A NON-CLUSTERED INDEX USING SQL SERVER MANAGEMENT STUDIO

GET READY. Before you begin, be sure to launch the SQL Server Management Studio application and connect to the database you want to work with. Then, follow these steps.

1. Click the plus (+) icon to the left of the Databases folder in order to expand the folder. You should now see instances of many subfolders in your main Database folder, as shown in Figure 4-13.

Figure 4-13

Database folder

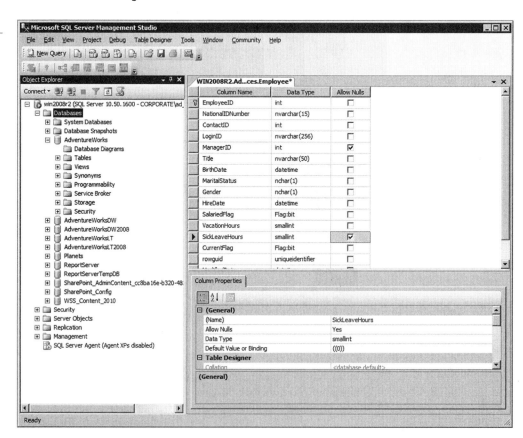

2. Click the plus (+) icon beside the database on which you would like to create an index, as shown in Figure 4-14. You should now see many different subfolders.

Figure 4-14

Creating an index

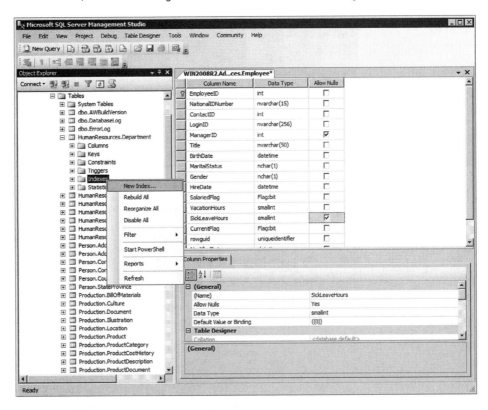

3. Click the plus (+) icon to the left of the Tables folder in order to expand it, as shown in Figure 4-15. You should now see a number of tables under the Tables folder.

Figure 4-15

Viewing the Tables folder

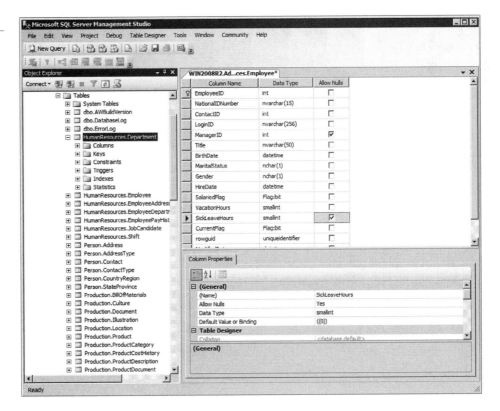

4. Right-click the Indexes subfolder and select New index from the pop-up menu that appears, as shown in Figure 4-16.

Figure 4-16

New Index menu

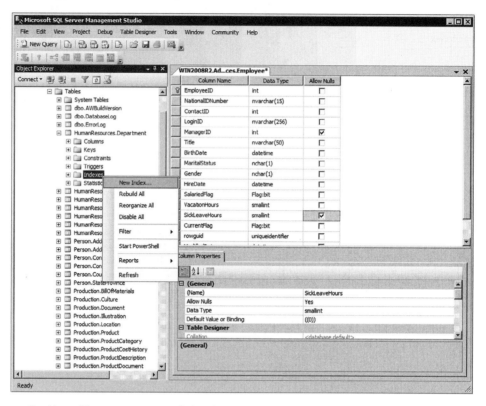

5. You will now see a new dialog box appear, the New Index properties box, for which you can input the desired inputs. This is where you would select whether the index you are creating is to be clustered or non-clustered (as shown in Figure 4-17).

Figure 4-17

New Index property box

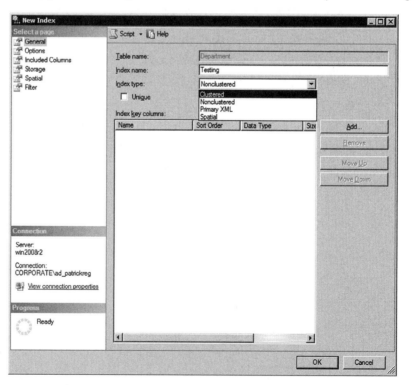

PAUSE. Leave the SSMS interface open for the next exercise.

For an idea of what a clustered index's Properties dialog box may look like, see Figure 4-18.

Figure 4-18

Clustered index property box

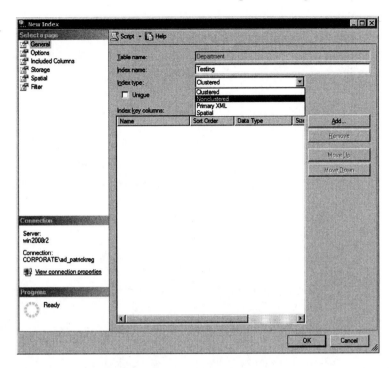

When looking at the example clustered index, note that you cannot add another index. Herein lies, as mentioned previously, the importance of ensuring you pick the right key to act as your clustered index key: This is your primary sorting index for the table, and you cannot have two clustered indexes per table.

However, on a table with a non-clustered index, you can add multiple table columns to the index key, as shown in Figure 4-19.

Figure 4-19

Non-clustered index property box

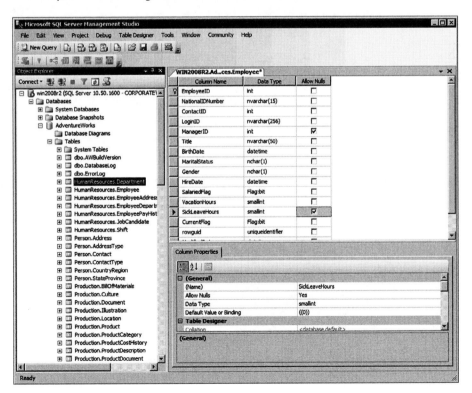

SKILL SUMMARY

IN THIS LESSON, YOU LEARNED THE FOLLOWING:

- Normalization, in a nutshell, is the elimination of redundant data to save space.
- In the first normalized form (1NF), the data is in an entity format, which basically means that the following three conditions must be met: the table must have no duplicate records, the table must not have multi-valued attributes, and the entries in the column or attribute must be of the same data type.
- The second normal form (2NF) ensures that each attribute does in fact describe the entity.
- The third normal form (3NF) checks for transitive dependencies. A transitive dependency is similar to a partial dependency in that they both refer to attributes that are not fully dependent on a primary key.
- The fourth normal form (4NF) involves two independent attributes brought together to form a primary key along with a third attribute.
- The fifth normal form (5NF) provides the method for designing complex relationships involving multiple (usually three or more) entities.
- Three different types of constraints available within SQL Server can help you maintain database integrity: primary keys, foreign keys, and composite (unique) keys.
- A unique key constraint allows you to enforce the uniqueness property of columns, in addition to a primary key within a table.
- Perhaps the most important concept in designing any database table is that it has a primary key—an attribute or set of attributes that can be used to uniquely identify each row.
- Every table must have a primary key; without a primary key, it's not a valid table. By definition, a primary key must be unique and must have a value that is not null.
- In order to connect two tables, the primary key is replicated from the primary to secondary table, and all the key attributes duplicated from the primary table are known as the foreign key.
- A composite primary key occurs when you define more than one column as your primary key.
- The primary drawbacks to using indexes are the time it takes to build the indexes and the storage space the indexes require.
- When you begin implementing indexes, it is important to remember that each table can have only one clustered index that defines how SQL Server will sort the data stored inside it, because that data can be sorted in only one way.
- A non-clustered index contains the non-clustered index key values, and each of those keys has a pointer to a data row that contains the key value.

■ Knowledge Assessment

True or False

Circle T if the statement is true or F if the statement is false.

T | F   **1.** Creating a primary key satisfies the first normal form.

T | F   **2.** Tables in a database must satisfy all five normal forms in order to maximize performance.

T | F   **3.** A primary key can contain NULL values.

T | F   **4.** A clustered index usually improves performance when inserting data.

T | F   **5.** A table can contain only one clustered index.

Fill in the Blank

Complete the following sentences by writing the correct word or words in the blanks provided.

1. Normalization is the elimination of redundant data to save _____.

2. The value of a primary key must be _____.

3. A foreign key works in conjunction with primary key or unique constraints to enforce _____ between tables.

4. Add an index to one or more columns to speed up data _____.

5. Values in a clustered index are _____.

Multiple Choice

Circle the letter that corresponds to the best answer.

1. Which of the following is not a constraint?
   a. CHECK
   b. DEFAULT
   c. UNIQUE
   d. INDEX

2. Which of the following things can help speed data retrieval?
   a. A DEFAULT constraint
   b. A primary key constraint
   c. A clustered index
   d. A foreign key constraint

3. Which of the following statements are true?
   a. A greater number of narrow tables (with fewer columns) is a characteristic of a normalized database.
   b. A few wide tables (with more columns) are characteristic of a normalized database.
   c. Indexes allow faster data retrieval.
   d. Optimal database performance can be achieved by indexing every column in a table.

4. Which of the following statements is not true with regard to foreign keys?
   a. A foreign key is a combination of one or more columns used to establish and enforce a link between the data in two tables.
   b. You can create a foreign key by defining a foreign key constraint when you create or alter a table.
   c. A foreign key enforces referential integrity by ensuring only valid data is stored.
   d. A table can contain only one foreign key.

5. Consider using a clustered index when:
   a. Columns contain a large number of distinct values
   b. Columns are accessed sequentially
   c. Columns undergo frequent changes
   d. Queries return large result sets

6. Which normal form ensures that each attribute describes the entity?
   a. 1NF
   b. 2NF
   c. 3NF
   d. 4NF

7. Which of the following could not be used as a primary key?
   a. A Social Security number
   b. An address
   c. An employee number
   d. The serial number of an electronic component

8. How many clustered indexes can you have for a database?
   a. 1
   b. 2
   c. 4
   d. 8

9. What is the name for the situation in which more than one columns act as a primary key?
   a. Composite primary key
   b. Escalating key
   c. Foreign key
   d. Constraint key

10. When you define a primary key, you have met the criteria for:
    a. 1NF
    b. 2NF
    c. 3NF
    d. 4NF

■ Competency Assessment

Scenario 4-1: Looking at 1NF

Your boss walks up to you and hands you a USB flash drive with the following database:

Model	Specs
PC-1000	Dell OptiPC 200XD, 2.0 Ghz, 512mb RAM, 40 GB HD
PC-1250	Dell SlimPC 400LX, 2.25Ghz, 2gb RAM, 160GB HD
PC-1500	Dell OptiPC 300XD 1.5Ghz, 4gb RAM, 200 GN HD

Your boss asks you if anything is wrong with the database and, if so, what should be done with it. How should you respond?

Scenario 4-2: Comparing Clustered and Non-Clustered Indexes

Your boss wants to speed things up on the company's database server. Therefore, he is thinking of having you create a couple of indexes. He asks you to explain the advantages and disadvantages of creating a clustered index versus a non-clustered index. How should you respond?

■ Proficiency Assessment

Scenario 4-3: Creating a Clustered Index

You are a database administrator for the AdventureWorks Corporation. You recently created some databases, and you've just realized how large the databases will become in the future. Therefore, you need to create a new clustered index to help with overall performance.

Using the SSMS interface, what steps would you use to create a new clustered index on the name column for the AdventureWorks database?

Scenario 4-4: Creating a Clustered Index Using Transact-SQL

As a database administrator, you need to increase the performance of the PlanetsID table, so you decide to create a clustered index. But instead of using SSMS, you decide to use queries to perform this task. Therefore, you create a new PlanetsID database using the following commands within SMMS:

```
IF EXISTS (SELECT * FROM sys.objects
WHERE object_id = OBJECT_ID(N'[dbo] . [PlanetsID]
   AND type in (N'U'))
USE AdventureWorks2008
DROP TABLE [dbo].[PlanetsID]
GO
USE [AdventureWorks2008]
GO
   CREATE TABLE [dbo].[PlanetsID](
   [ID] [int] NOT NULL,
   [Item] [int] NOT NULL,
   [Value] [int] NOT NULL
) ON [PRIMARY]
GO
INSERT INTO PlanetsID VALUES (4, 23, 66)
INSERT INTO PlanetsID VALUES (1, 12, 59)
INSERT INTO PlanetsID VALUES (3, 66, 24)
SELECT * FROM PlanetID
GO
```

You should now see the following output in the results pane (below the Query Editor Window):

```
ID      Item      Value
4       23        66
1       12        59
3       66        24
```

Now that you have a database with data, what steps would you use to create a clustered index based on the ID column?

5 LESSON

Administering a Database

OBJECTIVE DOMAIN MATRIX

SKILLS/CONCEPTS	MTA EXAM OBJECTIVE	MTA EXAM OBJECTIVE NUMBER
Securing Databases	Understand database security concepts.	5.1
Backing Up and Restoring Databases	Understand database backups and restores.	5.2

KEY TERMS

authentication

backup

base

data backup

database security

differential backup

full backup

guest user

incremental backup

log backup

login

permission

restore

sa account

server roles

sysadmin

user account

After you create the new table for the database that contains the second Washington store's inventory and sales data, your boss asks you to ensure that the store's employees are logging in to the correct database for their store data. She also requests that you work on and implement a backup plan for each store's information. Per your boss's request, you look at implementing both a full backup and an incremental backup schedule, as well as defining a new security schema.

The usefulness of a database depends in large part on the security of the information it contains. Therefore, as a database administrator, you must have a clear understanding of how permissions are granted so that users can access only certain tables or databases. In addition, you must be familiar with how and when to back up and restore a database.

Securing Databases

All database administrators must understand the need to secure a database, what objects can be secured, and what objects should be secured, as well as the importance of user accounts and roles.

It's common practice to first develop a database and then worry about the security of that database. Although there's no point in applying security while a database is in the process of being designed, the project will ultimately be beneficial if you consider your security plan sooner rather than later. Security, like every other aspect of a database project, must be carefully designed, implemented, and tested. Also, because security may affect the execution of some procedures, it must be taken into account when a project's code is being developed.

A simple security plan with only a few roles and all IT users designated as sysadmins may suffice for a small organization, but larger organizations—such as the military, banks, or international corporations—require a more complex security plan that's designed and implemented with heavy security in place. Regardless of an organization's size, the end result of its *database security* should be to ensure that users' assigned rights and responsibilities are enforced through a security plan.

Within a database, a *permission* is used to grant an entity (such as a user) access to an object (such as another user or a database). The security model within Microsoft SQL Server is very complex, so great thought must be given to applying appropriate user roles and permissions. The SQL Server security model is based on what are referred to as "securables"; in this model, different objects (defined as databases, tables, logins, users, and roles) can be granted permissions to access different securables.

A *login* or logon is the process by which individual access to a computer system is controlled by identification of the user through the credentials he or she provides. The most common login method involves supplying both a username and password. A *user account* is a logical representation of a person within an electronic system.

It is important to be aware of the rights and permissions associated with each object in a database because it's possible to inadvertently grant administrative rights to objects or users that should not have them. Within SQL Server, users are assigned to roles, which may in turn grant permission to objects, as illustrated in Figure 5-1. Note that each object has an owner, and ownership also affects permissions.

Figure 5-1

Planning roles and permissions

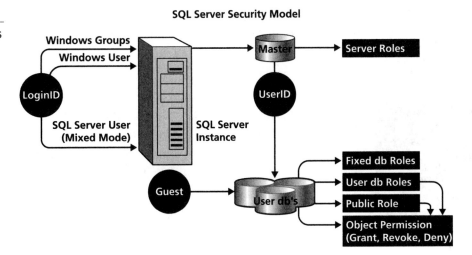

CERTIFICATION READY
What roles are assigned to a Microsoft SQL Server, and what roles are assigned to a SQL database?
5.1

An overview of the SQL Server security model shows that users are first authenticated to the server, followed by the databases, and finally the objects within the databases. In the diagram, the circles represent how the user is identified.

Understanding Server-Level Security

> In the security model for a SQL Server, there are three different methods by which a user can be initially identified.

TAKE NOTE*

Users can login to a SQL Server using a Windows domain login, a username login, or a SQL Server login.

The three different methods by which a user can be initially identified include:

- Windows user login
- Membership in a Windows user group
- SQL Server-specific login (if the server uses mixed-mode security)

It is important to remember that at the SQL Server level, where the database resides, users are known by their login names. This can be a SQL Server login, a Windows domain login, or a username login.

Once a user logs into the server and is subsequently verified, that user now has whatever server-level administration rights he or she has been granted via fixed server roles. (These concepts will be discussed in greater depth later in this lesson.)

Remember, if you add a user to the *sysadmin* role, that user now has full access to every server function, database, and object for that server. With full access, the user can now grant other users permission to all server securables, and he or she can perform a variety of system-level actions, such as adding his or her network login ID to be mapped to a specific database user ID. Thus, the sysadmin role is a powerful one, and you must be sure not to grant it to the wrong user login. Users who lack the sysadmin level of access can't alter database server configurations or grant access where they shouldn't be able to. It is possible for users who have not been granted direct access to a database to gain access using the "guest" user account—and with this account, they can make limited changes within the database server.

Understanding Database-Level Security

> Even though a user may belong to a fixed database role and have certain administrative-level permissions, he or she still cannot access data without first being granted permission to database objects (e.g., tables, stored procedures, views, functions).

TAKE NOTE*

Certain database fixed roles can also affect object access, such as the right to read to and write from the database.

All users are automatically members of the public standard database role, but user-defined roles are custom roles that serve as groups. These roles may then be granted permission to a database object, and users may be assigned to a database user-defined role.

Each object's permission is assigned through granting, denying, or revoking user login permissions:

CERTIFICATION READY
What is the primary permission that gives a user full permission to all databases? What is the primary permission that gives a user full permission to only a single database?
5.1

- Granting permission means that a user can access the object.
- Denying permission overrides a granted permission.
- Revoking a permission removes the permission that has been assigned, regardless of whether it was a denied permission or a granted permission.

A user may have multiple permission paths to an object (e.g., individually, through a standard database role, and through the public role). If any of these paths are denied, then the user is blocked from accessing the object.

Understanding Windows Security

> Because SQL Server is an environment within the Windows Server system, one of your primary security concerns should be ensuring that the Windows Server itself is secure.

Because SQL Server databases often support websites, you need to be sure that all firewalls and other Internet server applications are detailed and considered when constructing your security plan. You must also be familiar with the different types of SQL Server service accounts, as well as the basics of Windows authentication.

UNDERSTANDING SQL SERVER SERVICE ACCOUNTS

It is important to note that the SQL Server process itself requires permission to access files and directories, and it therefore requires a Windows account. Three different types of accounts are available for the SQL Server service account:

- **Local user account:** If you find that access to the network is not actually required, this is the perfect option to consider because a local user account cannot be used outside the server environment.
- **Local system account:** If you are using a single-server installation, you may wish to choose this account, because the SQL Server can use the local system account of the operating system for permission to the machine. The only drawback of using this account login is that it fails to provide the necessary network security credentials for databases because it has privileges inside the operating system that the administrator's account does not. This creates a potential security hole.
- **Domain user account:** This is the recommended login account because the SQL Server can then use the Windows account specifically created for it. You can then grant administrator rights to the SQL Server account.

UNDERSTANDING WINDOWS AUTHENTICATION

Authentication is the act of establishing or confirming a user or system identity. Windows Authentication mode is superior to mixed mode because users need not learn yet another password and because this mode leverages the security design of the network.

Using Windows Authentication means that users must have a valid Windows account in order to be recognized by SQL Server. The Windows SID (security identifier) is passed to SQL Server. Windows Authentication is very robust in that it will authenticate not only Windows users, but also users within Windows user groups.

When a Windows user group is accepted as a SQL Server login, any Windows user who is a member of that group can be authenticated by SQL Server. Access, roles, and permissions can be assigned to the Windows user group, and they will apply to any user in that group.

SQL Server also knows the actual Windows username for each user, so the application can gather audit information at both the user level and the group level.

ADDING A NEW WINDOWS LOGIN

Windows users are created and managed in various places in different versions of Windows. In Windows Vista and newer versions, local users can be managed by selecting Control Panel > Administrative Tools > Computer Management. Domain users are managed with tools such as the Active Directory Users and Computers snap-in.

Once users exist in the Windows user list or the Windows domain, SQL Server can recognize them.

ADD A NEW LOGIN TO SQL SERVER

GET READY. To add a new login to SQL Server through Object Explorer, follow these steps:

1. In SSMS, open and right-click the Security folder, select New and Select User, as shown in Figure 5-2.

Figure 5-2

Adding a new user

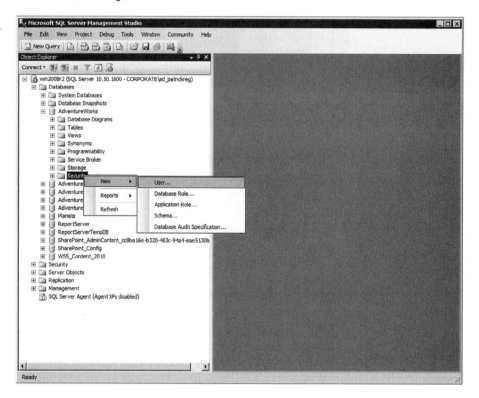

2. In the General page of the Database User, (as shown in Figure 5-3) type in the name of the user or you can use the Search (...) button to locate the Windows user.

Figure 5-3

Choosing a user name

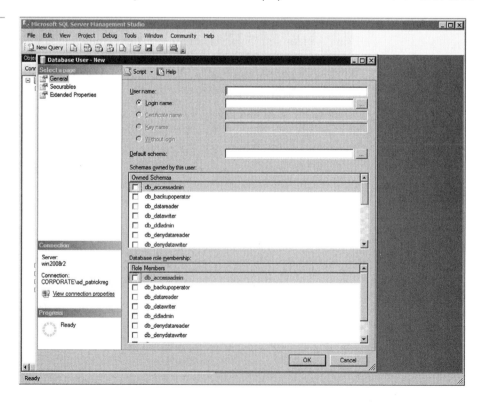

3. You may enter a username or group name or use the Browse button to search for a user, as shown in Figures 5-4 and 5-5. Windows users are managed and assigned to different Windows groups using the Computer Management tool.

Figure 5-4

Browsing for existing users

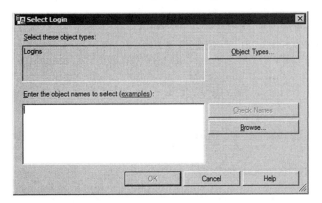

Figure 5-5

SQL Server logins

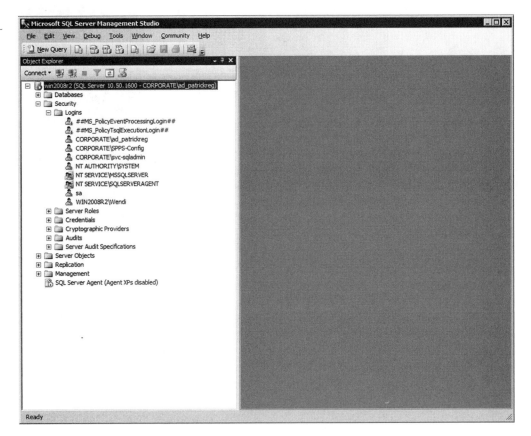

4. Click OK to save and close the Database User – New dialog box.

The user may be assigned a default database and language at the bottom of the SQL Server Login Properties dialog box, but note that assigning a default database to a user does not automatically grant access to that database. The user may be granted access to databases in the Database Access tab.

To create a login using Transact-SQL syntax so that you can add a Windows user or group, run the **CREATE LOGIN** command. Be sure to use the full Windows username, including the domain name, of the user you are trying to add, as follows:

```
CREATE LOGIN 'XPS\Joe'
```

TAKE NOTE *

A user can be granted access to databases in the Database Access tab.

If you want to create and edit user logins at the server level, use the General page of the Login/ New Dialog box. The Login dialog box is also used to manage existing users. To access the Login dialog box, just double-click the user.

REMOVING A WINDOWS LOGIN

A Windows login can be removed from SQL Server through SSMS. To do so, select the security directory (much as you did to create a new user login) in Object Browser, then use the menu to find and delete the desired user (as shown in Figure 5-6). Of course, this doesn't delete the user from Windows; it only removes the user from SQL Server.

Figure 5-6

Deleting an existing user from SQL Server

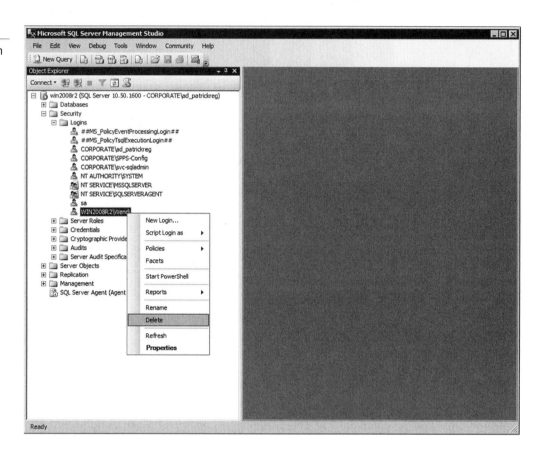

To remove a Windows user or group from SQL Server, you can also use the DROP LOGIN command, as in the following example:

```
DROP LOGIN 'XPS\Joe'
```

After running this command, the Windows user or group will continue to exist in Windows but will no longer be recognized by SQL Server.

Understanding SQL Authentication

SQL servers also support mixed mode, which allows you to connect to a SQL server using Windows authentication or SQL Server authentication. A SQL Server login account and related passwords are defined on the SQL server and are not related to Active Directory or Windows accounts.

Associated with SQL authentication is the *sa account*. The sa account is the built-in SQL administrator account associated with SQL authentication. Because SQL Authentication is less secure than Windows logins, avoiding mixed mode is recommended; however, it is available for backward compatibility.

Understanding Database Server Roles

There are three kinds of database server roles: fixed roles, the public role, and user-defined roles. Each of these roles is explored in greater depth in this section.

UNDERSTANDING FIXED SERVER ROLES

SQL Server includes fixed, predefined *server roles*. Primarily, these roles grant permission to perform certain server-related administrative tasks. A user may belong to multiple server roles.

The following fixed server roles are best used for delegating certain server administrative tasks:

- **Bulkadmin:** Can perform bulk insert operations.
- **Dbcreator:** Can create, alter, drop, and restore databases.
- **Diskadmin:** Can create, alter, and drop disk files.
- **Processadmin:** Can kill a running SQL Server process.
- **Securityadmin:** Can manage the logins for the server.
- **Serveradmin:** Can configure the server-wide settings, including setting up full-text searches and shutting down the server.
- **Setupadmin:** Can configure linked servers, extended stored procedures, and the startup stored procedure.
- **Sysadmin:** Can perform any activity in the SQL Server installation, regardless of any other permission setting. The sysadmin role even overrides denied permissions on an object.

The one user that SQL Server automatically creates during installation of the software is BUILTINS/Administrator, which includes all Windows users in the Windows Administration group and allows a choice of what groups or users are added during setup. The BUILTINS/ Administrators user can be deleted or modified as desired after installation.

If you add a user to the sysadmin role group, that user must reconnect to the SQL Server instance in order for the full capabilities of the sysadmin role to take effect.

Fixed server roles are set in SSMS in the Server Roles page of the Login Properties dialog box (see Figure 5-7).

Figure 5-7

Database Role Properties
dialog box

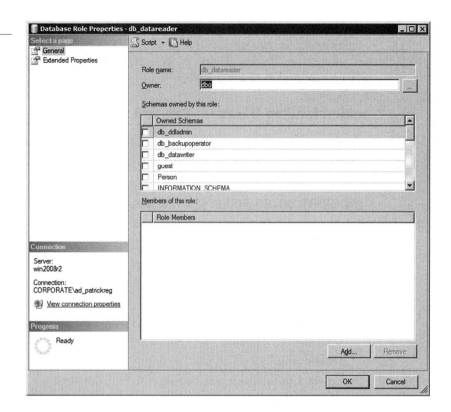

In Transact-SQL syntax, you can assign a user to different server roles by way of a stored procedure, as follows:

```
sp_addsrvrolemember
[ @loginame = ] 'login',
[ @rolename = ] 'role'
```

For example, the following code adds the user login "XPS\Lauren" to the sysadmin role:

```
EXEC sp_addsrvrolemember 'XPS\Lauren', 'sysadmin'
```

UNDERSTANDING THE PUBLIC ROLE

The public role is a fixed role, but it can have object permissions like a standard role. Every user is automatically a member of the public role and cannot be removed, so the public role serves as a baseline or minimum permission level.

UNDERSTANDING USER-DEFINED ROLES

Because you cannot modify the permissions assigned to a fixed server role, you may need to grant individual server permissions to a user that are not defined by a fixed server role. Such user-defined roles are typically employed for users who need to perform specific database functions but to whom you don't want to grant a role that would permit them do more than what they need to.

Granting Access to a Database

Users must be explicitly granted access to any user database. Because this establishes a many-to-many relationship between logins and the database, you can manage database access from either the login side or the database side.

When a login is granted access to a database, that login is also assigned a database username, which may be the same as the login name or may be some other name by which the login will be known within the database.

To grant access to a database from the login side using Object Explorer, use the User Mapping page of the Login Properties form (shown in Figure 5-8).

Figure 5-8

User Mapping page

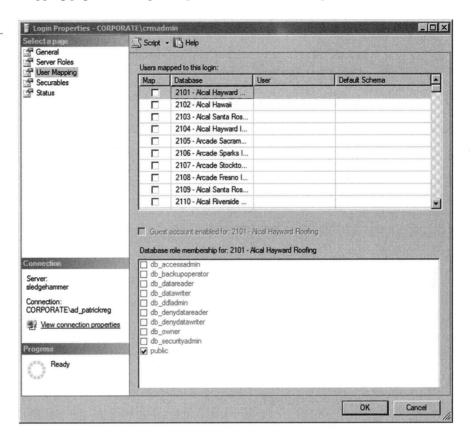

To grant access from the database point of view, use the New User Context Menu command under the Database > Security > Users node to open the Database User-New form. Enter the login to be added in the Login Name field. To search for a login, use the ellipsis (. . .) button. In the User Name field, you must enter a name by which the user will be known within the database.

You can use the Login Properties form to grant a login access to any database and to assign database roles.

A Transact-SQL command is also available to grant database access to a user. This command must be issued from within the database to which the user is to be granted access. The first parameter in the command syntax is the server login, and the second is the optional database username, as in the following example:

```
USE Family
CREATE USER 'XPS\Lauren', 'LRN'
```

Lauren now appears in the list of database users as LRN. To remove Lauren's database access, the system-stored procedure DROP USER requires her database username, not her server login name, as follows:

```
USE Family
DROP USER 'LRN'
```

The Login dialog box can be used to add a new user to the database or to manage a current user.

UNDERSTANDING GUEST LOGIN ACCOUNTS

Any user who wishes to access a database but who has not been declared a user within the database is automatically granted the privileges of the *guest user*, as long as the guest user account has been created. The guest user account is not actually created when a database is created; it must be specifically added either through SSMS or through a Transact-SQL statement, as shown here:

```
EXEC sp_adduser 'Guest'
```

Guest users must be removed from a database when they are no longer welcome, as they are a risk for a security breach.

UNDERSTANDING OBJECT SECURITY

If a user has access to a database, then permission to the individual database objects may be granted. Permission may be granted either directly to the user or to a standard role, with the user then assigned to the role.

Users may be assigned to multiple roles, so multiple security paths from a user to an object may exist.

Understanding Fixed Database Roles

SQL Server includes a few standard, or fixed, database roles. Like fixed server roles, these roles primarily organize administrative tasks. A user may belong to multiple fixed database roles.

In SQL Server, fixed database roles include the following:

- **db_accessadmin:** Authorizes a user to access the database, but not to manage database-level security.
- **db_backupoperator:** Allows a user to perform backups, checkpoints, and DBCC commands, but not restores. (Only server sysadmins can perform restores.)
- **db_datareader:** Authorizes a user to read all data in the database. This role is the equivalent of a grant on all objects, and it can be overridden by a deny permission.
- **db_datawriter:** Allows a user to write to all data in the database. This role is the equivalent of a grant on all objects, and it can be overridden by a deny permission.
- **db_ddladmin:** Authorizes a user to issue DDL commands (create, alter, drop).
- **db_denydatareader:** Permits a user to read from any table in the database. This overrides any object-level grant.
- **db_denydatawriter:** Blocks a user from modifying data in any table in the database. This overrides any object-level grant.
- **db_owner:** This is a special role that has all permissions in the database. This role includes all the capabilities of the other roles and differs from the dbo user role. This is not the database-level equivalent of the server sysadmin role because an object-level deny will override membership in this role.
- **db_securityadmin:** Permits a user to manage database-level security—including roles and permissions.

ASSIGNING FIXED DATABASE ROLES WITH SSMS

Fxed database roles can be assigned via SSMS using either of the following procedures:

- By adding the role to the user in the user's Database User Properties form, either as the user is being created or after the user exists.
- By adding the user to the role in the Database Role Properties dialog. To do so, select Roles under the database's Security node, then use the context menu to open the Properties form (see Figure 5-9).

ASSIGNING FIXED DATABASE ROLES WITH TRANSACT-SQL

In Transact-SQL code, you can add a user to a fixed database role by using the sp_addrole system stored procedure. For instance, the following example creates the database role auditors, which is owned by the db_securityadmin fixed database role:

```
USE AdventureWorks;
CREATE ROLE auditors AUTHORIZATION db_securityadmin;
GO
```

UNDERSTANDING APPLICATION ROLES

An application role is a database-specific role intended to allow an application to gain access regardless of its user. For example, if a specific Visual Basic (VB) program is used to search the Customer table and it doesn't handle user identification, that VB program can access SQL Server using a hard-coded application role. Thus, anyone using the VB application gains access to the database.

The Database Role Properties dialog box lists all users assigned to the current role.

ACCESSING THE DATABASE ROLES

GET READY. To add a user to a database role, follow these steps:

1. In SSMS, expand the database folder by clicking the appropriate plus (+) sign. Expand the Security folder, Expand Roles, and then expand the Database Roles folder.
2. Double-click the appropriate role to open the Properties dialog box.
3. To add or remove users from the role, use the Add and Remove buttons, respectively.

Understanding Object Permissions

Object permissions are permissions that allow a user to act on database objects, such as tables, stored procedures, and views.

Several specific types of object permissions exist:

- **Select:** The right to select data. Select permission can be applied to specific columns.
- **Insert:** The right to insert data.
- **Update:** The right to modify existing data. Update rights for which a WHERE clause is used require select rights as well. Update permission can be set on specific columns.
- **Delete:** The right to delete existing data.
- **DRI (References):** The right to create foreign keys with DRI.
- **Execute:** The right to execute stored procedures or user-defined functions.

Object permissions are assigned with the SQL DCL commands GRANT, REVOKE, and DENY. Permissions in SQL Server work just as they do in the operating system. SQL Server aggregates all the permissions a given user might have, whether assigned directly to the user or assigned through roles.

SQL Server gives the maximum of whatever permission has been granted. DENY is an exception to this rule, however. DENY functions as a trump card of sorts. In other words, if a DENY command has been issued anywhere, then, just as in Windows, the user is blocked. For instance, if a user can SELECT against a table directly assigned, but a role the user is a member of has a DENY for SELECT, then this user is blocked from issuing a SELECT against the table. Whether security is being managed from SSMS or from code, it's important to understand these three commands.

Granting object permission interacts with the server and database roles. The sysadmin server role is the ultimate security role, which has full access to all databases.

If a user does not have the sysadmin server role, the highest level object permission would be the Grant and Deny object permissions. However, Deny permission always has a higher priority than the Grant permission.

If your environment prohibits mixed-mode security, then the easiest way to check security is to right-click SQL Server Management Studio or Query Analyzer and use the RUN AS command to run as a different user; however, this requires the creation of dummy users in the Windows domain. Generally speaking, in a "production" Windows domain, most auditors would flag dummy users as an audit point. Because the workstations that belong to database administrators tend to belong in production domains, this recommendation won't work if the auditors are diligent.

 MODIFY AN OBJECT'S PERMISSIONS

GET READY. To access an object's permission, follow these steps to modify an object's permissions:

1. In SSMS, open the database and open the object that you want to manage. The object could be tables, views, stored procedures, or user-defined functions.

2. In the Object Browser, right-click the object and select Properties to open the Properties dialog for that object type.

3. Click the Permissions page to open the Object Properties dialog.

4. To add a user, click the Search button. Type in the name of the user you wish to add or click the Browse button to select the user. Click the OK button to close the Select Users or Roles dialog box.

5. Select the appropriate Grant to Deny permission. See Figure 5-9.

Figure 5-9

Granting Object Permissions

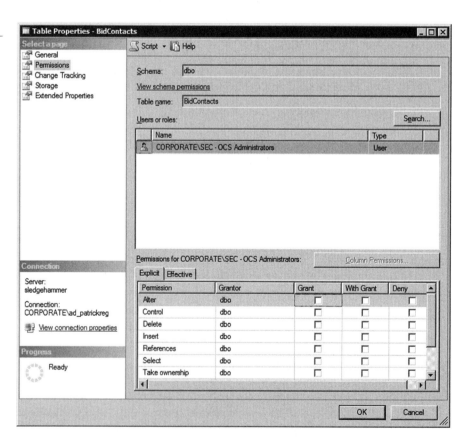

6. When done, click the OK button to close the Properties dialog box.

The top portion of the form is for selecting a user or role to assign or check permissions. The user must have access to the database to be selected.

As with setting statement permissions in the Database Properties Security tab, you can select grant, with grant, or deny. The object list at the top of the dialog box shows all the objects in the database. This list can be used to switch to other objects quickly without backing out of the form to the console and selecting a different object.

If the user or role has permission to a table, the Columns button opens the Column Permissions dialog. Select the user and click the button to set the columns permissions for that user. Only select and update permissions can be set at the column level, because inserts and deletes affect entire rows.

SETTING PERMISSIONS FROM THE USER LIST

Instead of granting the permission to a user from the properties of the object, you can also grant permissions to an object from the properties of the user. From the list of database users in SSMS, select a user and double-click, or select Properties from the right-click context menu. The Login Properties dialog box will appear, and it can be used to assign users to roles (as shown in Figure 5-10). The Securables page is used to assign or check object permissions. This dialog box is similar to the Permissions tab of the Database Object Properties dialog box.

Figure 5-10

Login Properties dialog box

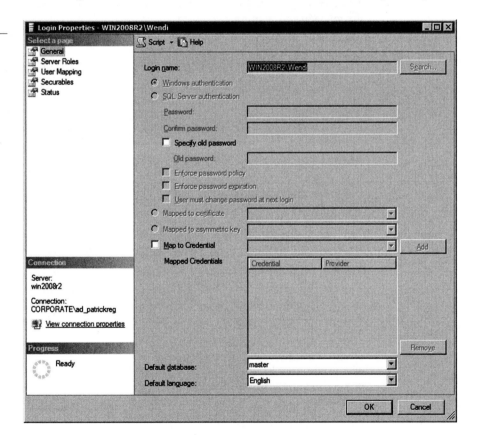

SETTING PERMISSIONS FROM THE ROLE LIST

The third way to control object permissions is from the database role. To open the Database Role Properties dialog box, double-click a role in the list of roles, or select Properties from the right-click context menu. The Database Role Properties dialog box can be used to assign users or other roles to a role, as well as to remove them from a role.

The Permissions button opens the Permissions dialog box for the role. This form operates like the other permission forms, except it is organized from the role's perspective.

GRANTING OBJECT PERMISSIONS WITH TRANSACT-SQL STATEMENTS

Using Transact-SQL, you can grant any object permissions to a database, table, view, or any other database object. The Transact-SQL statement to provide permission to an object for a specific user and his or her role is as follows:

```
GRANT Permission, Permission
ON Object
TO User/role, User/role
WITH GRANT OPTION
```

The assigned permission may be ALL, SELECT, INSERT, DELETE, REFERENCES, UPDATE, or EXECUTE. The role or username refers to the database username, any user-defined public role, or the public role. For example, the following code grants select permission to Joe for the Person table:

```
GRANT Select ON Emails TO Joe
```

The next example grants all permissions to the public role for the Marriage table:

```
GRANT All ON Contacts TO dbcreator
```

Multiple users or roles and multiple permissions may be listed in the command. For example, the following code grants select and update permission to the guest user and to LRN:

```
GRANT Select, Update ON Emails to Guest, LRN
```

The WITH GRANT option provides the ability to grant permission for an object. For example, the following command grants Joe permission both to select from the Email table and to grant select permission to others:

```
GRANT Select ON Email TO Joe WITH GRANT OPTION
```

Managing Roles

Roles can be created, managed, and removed via SSMS or by executing Transact-SQL statements. Of course, you should create roles and assign users to those roles only when needed.

MANAGING ROLES WITH TRANSACT-SQL STATEMENTS

Creating standard roles with code involves using the sp_addrole system stored procedure. A role's name can be up to 128 characters and cannot include a backslash, be null, or be an empty string. By default, the roles will be owned by the dbo user. However, you can assign the role of owner by adding a second parameter. The following code creates the manager role:

```
CREATE ROLE 'Manager'
```

The counterpart to creating a role is removing it. A role may not be dropped if any users are currently assigned to it. The sp_droprole system stored procedure will remove the role from the database, as in the following example:

```
DROP ROLE 'Manager'
```

Once a role has been created, users may be assigned to the role by means of the sp_addrolemember system stored procedure. For instance, the following code sample assigns Joe to the manager role:

```
EXEC sp_addrolemember 'Manager', 'Joe'
```

Not surprisingly, the system stored procedure sp_droprolemember removes a user from an assigned role. Thus, the following code frees Joe from the drudgery of management:

```
EXEC sp_dropRoleMember 'Manager', 'Joe'
```

UNDERSTANDING HIERARCHICAL ROLE STRUCTURES

If your security structure is complex, then a particularly powerful permissions-organization technique is to design a hierarchical structure of standard database roles. In other words, you can nest user-defined database roles. For example:

- The worker role may have limited access.
- The manager role may have all worker rights plus additional rights to look up tables.
- The administrator role may have all manager rights plus the right to perform other database administration tasks.

To accomplish this type of design, follow these steps:

1. Create the worker role and set its permissions.
2. Create the manager role and set its permissions. Add the manager role as a user to the worker role.
3. Create the admin role. Add the admin role as a user to the manager role.

The advantage of this type of security organization is that a change in the lower level affects all upper levels. As a result, administration is required in only one location, rather than dozens of locations.

Understanding Ownership Chains

In SQL Server databases, users often access data by going through one or several objects. Ownership chains apply to views, stored procedures, and user-defined functions.

There are many occasions where a database object will access another database object. For example:

- A program might call a stored procedure that then selects data from a table.
- A report might select from a view, which then selects from a table.
- A complex stored procedure might call several other stored procedures.

In these cases, the user must have permission to execute the stored procedure or select from the view.

Whether the user also needs permission to select from the underlying tables depends on the ownership chain from the object the user called to the underlying tables.

If the ownership chain is unbroken from the stored procedure to the underlying tables, then the stored procedure can execute using the permission of its owner. The user only needs permission to execute the stored procedure, and the stored procedure can use its owner's permission to access the underlying tables. Thus, the user doesn't require permission to the underlying tables.

Ownership chains are great for developing tight security where users execute stored procedures but aren't granted direct permission to any tables.

If the ownership chain is broken, meaning the owners of one object and the next lower object are different, then SQL Server checks the user's permission for every object accessed.

Reviewing a Sample Security Model

To give a few examples of permissions using the OBXKites database, Table 5-1 lists the permission settings of the standard database roles. Table 5-2 lists a few of the users and their roles.

Table 5-1

Permission settings for OBXKites

STANDARD ROLE	HIERARCHICAL ROLE	PRIMARY FILEGROUP TABLES	STATIC FILEGROUP TABLES	OTHER PERMISSIONS
IT	Sysadmin server role			
Clerk				Execute permissions for several stored procedures that read from and update required day-to-day tables.
Admin	Db_owner Database fixed role			
Customer		Select permissions		

Table 5-2

Users and their roles for OBXKites

USER	DATABASE STANDARD ROLES
Sammy	Admin
Joe	Public
LRN	IT DBA
Clerk Windows group (Betty, Tom, Martha, and Mary)	Clerk

With this security model, the following users can perform the following tasks:

- Betty, as a member of the Clerk role, can execute the application that executes stored procedures to retrieve and update data. Betty can also run select queries as a member of the Public role.
- LRN, as the IT DBA, can perform any task in the database as a member of the Sysadmin server role.
- Joe can run select queries as a member of the Public role.
- As a member of the Admin role, Sammy can execute all stored procedures. He can also manually modify any table using queries. Furthermore, as a member of the Admin role that includes the Db_owner role, Joe can perform any database administrative task and select or modify data in any table.
- Only LRN can restore from the backups. Backups are discussed in the next part of the lesson.

Backing Up and Restoring Databases

↓ THE BOTTOM LINE In this section, you'll explore various backup types (such as full and incremental), the importance of backups, and how to restore a database.

The purpose of a database *backup* is to have something to restore if data is lost during a business's daily routine. For example, a user may accidentally delete a table, or a database administrator may need to *restore* multiple tables on different servers in order to combine them into one database. The need for a database backup and restore plan is both immediate and far reaching.

Understanding Recovery Models

SQL Server offers several recovery models for each database. The recovery models determine how much data loss in case the server has problems and you need to restore the data from backup.

SQL Server offers three recovery models. They are:

- Simple Recovery
- Full Recovery
- Bulk-Logged

Simple Recovery requires the least administration since the transaction log backups are truncated on a regular basis.

Full Recovery allows you to restore to a point in time since the logs files record all SQL transactions and the time they were performed. The disadvantages of Full Recovery mode is that the logs can grow a lot. Therefore, when you perform full backups, you will need to shrink and truncate the logs.

The least used model used is Bulk-Logged. It is a compromise between the two. It allows good performance while using the least log space. However, you cannot do a point-in-time recovery.

Understanding Database Backups

The scope of a backup of data (a *data backup*) can be a whole database, a partial database, or a set of files or filegroups. For each of these, SQL Server supports full, differential, and incremental backups.

CERTIFICATION READY
What is the difference between a full backup and an incremental backup?
5.2

When you perform backups, you can choose the type of backup that is best for your environment. The type of backup is based on simplicity, time to perform a backup, and time to perform a restore.

- *Full backup:* A full backup contains all the data in a specific database or set of filegroups or files to allow recovering that data.
- *Differential backup:* A differential backup is based on the latest full backup of the data. This is known as the *base* of the differential, or the differential base. A differential backup contains only the data that has changed since the differential base. Typically, differential backups that are taken fairly soon after the base backup are smaller and faster to

create than the base of a full backup. Therefore, using differential backups can speed up the process of making frequent backups to decrease the risk of data loss. Usually, a differential base is used by several successive differential backups. At restore time, the full backup is restored first, followed by the most recent differential backup.

- *Incremental backup:* An incremental backup is based on the last backup of the data. An incremental backup contains only the data that has changed since the last full or incremental backup. Incremental backups are smaller and faster to create than full backups and differential backups. At restore time, the full backup is restored first, followed by each incremental backup following the full backup.

Over time, as a database is updated, the amount of data that is included in differential backups increases. This makes the backup slower to create and to restore. Eventually, another full backup must be created to provide a new differential base for another series of differential backups.

After the first data backup, under the full recovery model or bulk-logged recovery model, regular transaction log backups (or *log backups*) are required. Each log backup covers the part of the transaction log that was active when the backup was created, and the log backup includes all log records that were not backed up in a previous log backup.

Database backups are easy to use and are recommended whenever database size allows. Table 5-3 shows the types of database backups supported by SQL Server.

Table 5-3

Types of database backups supported by Microsoft SQL

BACKUP TYPE	DESCRIPTION
Database backup	A full backup of the whole database. Database backups represent the whole database at the time the backup finished.
Differential database backups	A backup of all files in the database. This backup contains only the data that were modified since the most recent database backup of each file.

UNDERSTANDING PARTIAL AND DIFFERENTIAL BACKUPS

Partial and differential partial backups are designed to provide more flexibility for backing up databases that contain some read-only filegroups under the simple recovery model. However, these backups are supported by all recovery models. Table 5-4 shows the types of partial backups supported by SQL Server.

Table 5-4

Types of partial backups supported by Microsoft SQL

BACKUP TYPE	DESCRIPTION
Partial backup	A backup of all the full data in the primary filegroup, every read/write filegroup, and any optionally specified read-only files or filegroups. A partial backup of a read-only database contains only the primary filegroup.
Differential partial backup	A backup that contains only the data that were modified since the most recent partial backup of the same set of filegroups.

UNDERSTANDING FILE BACKUPS

The files in a database can also be backed up and restored individually. Using file backups can increase the speed of recovery by letting you restore only damaged files without restoring the rest of the database. For example, if a database consists of several files that are located on different disks and one disk fails, only the file on the failed disk will need to be restored. However, planning and restoring file backups can be complex; therefore, file backups should be used only where they clearly add value to your restore plan. Table 5-5 shows the types of file backups supported by SQL Server.

Table 5-5

Types of file backups

BACKUP TYPE	DESCRIPTION
File backup	A full backup of all the data in one or more files or filegroups. Important: Under the simple recovery model, file backups are basically restricted to read-only secondary filegroups. You can create a file backup of a read/write filegroup, but before you can restore the read/write file backup, you must set the filegroup to read-only and take a differential read-only file backup.
Differential file backups	A backup of one or more files that contain data extents that were changed since the most recent full backup of each file. Note: Under the simple recovery model, this assumes that the data has been changed to read-only since the full backup.

Understanding Backup Devices

SQL Server backups are created on backup devices such as disk files or tape media. You can append new backups to any existing backups on a device, or you can overwrite any existing backups.

SCHEDULING BACKUPS

Performing a backup operation has minimal effect on transactions that are running; therefore, backup operations can be run during regular operations. During a backup operation, SQL Server copies the data directly from the database files to the backup devices. The data is not changed, and transactions that are running during the backup are never delayed. Therefore, you can perform a SQL Server backup with minimal effect on production workloads.

Understanding Database Restores

SQL Server supports a variety of restore scenarios, each of which is outlined in the following section.

Restore scenarios possible in SQL Server include the following:

- **Complete database restore:** Restores an entire database, beginning with a full database backup, which may be followed by restoring a differential database backup (and log backups).

- **File restore:** Restores a file or filegroup in a multi-filegroup database. After a full file restore, a differential file backup can be restored.
- **Page restore:** Restores individual pages.
- **Piecemeal restore:** Restores a database in stages, beginning with the primary filegroup and one or more secondary filegroups.
- **Recovery only:** Recovers data that is already consistent with the database and needs only to be made available.
- **Transaction log restore:** Under the full or bulk-logged recovery model, since the logs record each transaction, restoring from log backups is required to reach a desired recovery point.
- **Create a mirror database:** When you have a mirror database, you have duplicate databases on multiple servers. When information is written to one server, it is automatically replicated to the second server.
- **Create and maintain a standby server:** When you have a standby server, you are using an active-passive cluster that consists of two or more servers. When the active server fails, the passive server will become the active server, allowing for minimum downtime.

USING THE SSMS

To restore data through the graphical interface tool, follow these steps.

 RESTORING DATA

GET READY. Before you begin, be sure to launch the SQL Server Management Studio application and connect to the database you wish to work with. Then, follow these steps:

1. After you connect to the appropriate instance of the Microsoft SQL Server Database Engine, in Object Explorer, click the server name to expand the server tree.
2. Expand **Databases.** Depending on the database, either select a user database or expand **System Databases** and then select a system database.
3. Right-click the database, point to **Tasks**, then click **Restore.**
4. Click **Database**, which opens the **Restore Database** dialog box.
5. On the **General** page, the name of the restoring database appears in the **To database** list box. To create a new database, enter its name in the list box.
6. In the **To a point in time** text box, either retain the default (*the most recent possible*) or select a specific date and time by clicking the browse button, which opens the **Point in Time Restore** dialog box.
7. To specify the source and location of the backup sets to restore, click one of the following options:
   - **From database:** Enter a database name in the list box.
   - **From device:** Click the browse button, which opens the **Specify Backup** dialog box. In the **Backup media** list box, select one of the listed device types. To select one or more devices for the **Backup location** list box, click **Add.**

     After you add the devices you want to the **Backup location** list box, click **OK** to return to the **General** page.
8. In the **Select the backup sets to restore** grid, select the backups to restore. This grid displays the backups available for the specified location. By default, a recovery plan is suggested. To override the suggested recovery plan, change the selections in the grid. Any backups that depend on a deselected backup are deselected automatically.
9. To view or select the advanced options, click **Options** in the **Select a page** pane.

10. In the **Restore options** panel, you can choose any of the following options, if appropriate for your situation:
    - Overwrite the existing database.
    - Preserve the replication settings.
    - Prompt before restoring each backup.
    - Restrict access to the restored database.

11. Optionally, you can restore the database to a new location by specifying a new restore destination for each file in the **Restore the database files as** grid.

12. The **Recovery state** panel determines the state of the database after the restore operation. The default behavior isLeave the database ready to use by rolling back the uncommitted transactions. Additional transaction logs cannot be restored (RESTORE WITH RECOVERY). (Choose this option only if you are restoring all the necessary backups at this point.)

13. Alternatively, you can choose either of the following options:
    - Leave the database non-operational, and do not roll back the uncommitted transactions. Additional transaction logs can be restored (RESTORE WITH NO RECOVERY).
    - Leave the database in read-only mode. Undo uncommitted transactions, but save the undo actions in a standby file so that recovery effects can be reverted (RESTORE WITH STANDBY).

CERTIFICATION READY
Do you understand database backups and restores?
5.2

USING THE RESTORE COMMAND

The Transact-SQL RESTORE command enables you to perform the following restore scenarios:

- Restore an entire database from a full database backup (a complete restore).
- Restore part of a database (a partial restore).
- Restore specific files or filegroups to a database (a file restore).
- Restore specific pages to a database (a page restore).
- Restore a transaction log onto a database (a transaction log restore).
- Revert a database to the point in time captured by a database snapshot.

For example, to restore the database using the specified file, you would execute the following command:

```
RESTORE DATABASE name_of_database FROM DISK = 'name of backup'
  GO
```

For example, to restore the AdventureWorks database using the C:\AdventureWorks.BAK backup, you would execute the following command:

```
RESTORE DATABASE AdventureWorks FROM DISK = 'C:\AventureWorks.BAK'
  GO
```

For more information on using the RESTORE command, refer to the following website:

http://msdn.microsoft.com/en-us/library/ms186858.aspx

SKILL SUMMARY

IN THIS LESSON, YOU LEARNED THE FOLLOWING:

- The end result of database security is to ensure that the rights and responsibilities given to users are enforced.

- A permission is used to grant an entity (such as a user) access to an object (such as another user or a database).

- A login or logon is the process by which individual access to a computer system is controlled by identification of the user using credentials provided by the user. The most common login method involves supplying a username and password.

- A user account is a logical representation of a person within an electronic system.

- Even though a user may belong to a fixed database role and have certain administrative-level permissions, a user still cannot access data without first being granted permission to the database object themselves (e.g., tables, stored procedures, views, functions).

- Each object's permission is assigned by granting, revoking, or denying user login permissions.

- Authentication is the act of establishing or confirming a user or system identity.

- Windows Authentication mode is superior to mixed mode because users don't need to learn yet another password and because it leverages the security design of the network.

- The sa account is the built-in SQL administrator account associated with SQL authentication.

- SQL Server includes fixed, predefined server roles. Primarily, these roles grant permission to perform certain server-related administrative tasks.

- The sysadmin role can perform any activity in the SQL Server installation, regardless of any other permission setting. The sysadmin role even overrides denied permissions on an object.

- The public role is a fixed role, but it can have object permissions like a standard role. Every user is automatically a member of the public role and cannot be removed, so the public role serves as a baseline or minimum permission level.

- Users must be explicitly granted access to any user database.

- The db_owner is a special role that has all permissions in the database.

- An application role is a database-specific role intended to allow an application to gain access regardless of the user.

- The purpose of a database backup is to have something to restore if data is lost during a business's daily routine.

- A full backup contains all the data in a specific database or set of filegroups or files to allow recovering that data.

- Differential backup only backs up data since the last full backup.

- Incremental backup only backs up data since the last full or incremental backup.

- When you restore from differential backup, you must first restore the preceding full backup and then restore the last differential backup.

- When you restore from an incremental backup, you must first restore the preceding full backup and then restore each incremental backup since the full backup in order.

Knowledge Assessment

True or False

Circle T if the statement is true or F if the statement is false

T | F   **1.** A user must have permissions to access the files that make up a database in order to use the database.

T | F   **2.** Use the CREATE LOGIN statement to allow a Windows account to access SQL-Server.

T | F   **3.** Any DENY permission always overrides a granted permission.

T | F   **4.** Use the CREATE ROLE statement to create new roles within a database.

T | F   **5.** Multiple differential backups must be restored in the same order as originally created.

Fill in the Blank

Complete the following sentences by writing the correct word or words in the blanks provided.

1. SQL Server uses Windows _____ to verify that a user is valid before access is allowed.

2. A differential backup contains only the data that has _____ since the differential base.

3. All users are automatically a member of the _____ database role.

4. Use the _____ command to allow users to access objects within the database.

5. Use the _____ command to recover data that was accidentally deleted by a user.

Multiple Choice

Circle the letter that corresponds to the best answer.

1. Which of the following is not a Transact-SQL command to manage permissions?
   a. GRANT
   b. REVOKE
   c. PERMIT
   d. DENY

2. Which of the following is not a level of security supported by SQL Server?
   a. Server
   b. Database
   c. Table
   d. Task

3. Which of the following is not a database permission that can be applied to objects?
   a. DROP
   b. SELECT
   c. INSERT
   d. UPDATE

4. Which of the following are supported database restore scenarios?
   a. Restore an entire database from a full backup.
   b. Restore an entire database from a series of partial backups.
   c. Restore part of a database using partial backups.
   d. Restore specific files used by the database.

5. Which of the following is not a type of backup supported by SQL Server?
   a. Full
   b. Differential
   c. File
   d. Device

6. What is a built-in SQL account used in mixed mode that has full access to the SQL server?
   a. fulladmin
   b. sa
   c. admin
   d. administrator

7. You just hired a new database administrator and you want to give her full access to your SQL server. What role should you assign?
   a. diskadmin
   b. securityAdmin
   c. sysadmin
   d. db_owner

8. What role gives full access to an individual database?
   a. db_owner
   b. db_accessadmin
   c. db_securityadmin
   d. db_ddladmin

9. The best method of data recovery is to:
   a. backup, backup, backup
   b. use RAID
   c. use UPS
   d. use redundant NICs

10. What mode allows both Windows and SQL account logins?
    a. Any
    b. Full
    c. Shared
    d. Mixed

■ Competency Assessment

Scenario 5-1: Looking at SQL Server Security

Your boss took a SQL course in college a few years ago. He asks if he can logon to the SQL server with the sa account so that he can look at the databases and run a few queries. Unfortunately, you tell him that the sa account is not available on the server. He wants to know why, and he wants to know what he can use to access the databases. What should you tell your boss?

Scenario 5-2: Using Full and Incremental Backups

You have six large databases, each being at least 2 GB. You need to make sure that you back up the databases each night in case you have a disaster and must recover them from backup. Because each database takes two hours to back up and you only have a six-hour window in which to do backups each day, what would you recommend as a backup solution?

Proficiency Assessment

Scenario 5-3: Backing Up a Database

Because you are going to do some maintenance on your databases and database servers, you decide to perform a backup. Using SQL Server Management Studio, what steps would you take to make a full backup of the AdventureWorks database and save it to your hard drive?

Scenario 5-4: Restoring a Backup (Complete Restore)

When you were doing some database maintenance, one of your tables got corrupted. Thankfully, you were smart enough to backup the database. Using SSMS, what steps would you take to restore the database that you backed up in the last exercise?

Exam Objective	Exam Objective Number	Lesson Number
Understanding Core Database Concepts		
Understand how data is stored in tables.	1.1	1
Understand relational database concepts.	1.2	1
Understand data manipulation language (DML).	1.3	1
Understand data definition language (DDL).	1.4	1
Creating Database Objects		
Choose data types.	2.1	2
Understand tables and how to create them.	2.2	2
Create views.	2.3	2
Create stored procedures and functions.	2.4	2
Manipulating Data		
Select data.	3.1	3
Insert data.	3.2	3
Update data.	3.3	3
Delete data.	3.4	3
Understanding Data Storage		
Understand normalization.	4.1	4
Understand primary, foreign, and composite keys.	4.2	4
Understand indexes.	4.3	4
Administering a Database		
Understand database security concepts.	5.1	5
Understand database backups and restore.	5.2	5

Notes

Notes

Notes

Notes

Notes

Notes

Notes

Notes

Notes

Notes

Notes